Disney Songs for HARMONICA

30 Favorites Arranged for Diatonic Harmonica

Arranged by Eric J. Plahna

The following songs are the property of:
Bourne Co.
Music Publishers
5 West 37th Street
New York, NY 10018

BABY MINE
HEIGH-HO
I'M WISHING
I'VE GOT NO STRINGS
WHO'S AFRAID OF THE BIG BAD WOLF?
WITH A SMILE AND A SONG

ISBN 978-1-4950-7956-6

DISTRIBUTED BY

7777 W. BLUEMOUND RD. P.O. BOX 13819 MILWAUKEE, WI 53213

Visit Hal Leonard Online at
www.halleonard.com

CONTENTS

HARMONICA NOTATION LEGEND

Harmonica music can be notated two different ways: on a *musical staff*, and in *tablature*.

THE MUSICAL STAFF shows pitches and rhythms and is divided by bar lines into measures. Pitches are named after the first seven letters of the alphabet.

TABLATURE graphically represents the harmonica music. Each note will be accompanied by a number, 1 through 10, indicating what hole you are to play. The arrow that follows indicates whether to blow or draw. (All examples are shown using a C diatonic harmonica.)

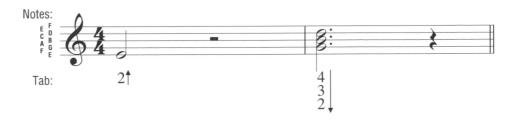

Blow (exhale) into 2nd hole.

Draw (inhale) 2nd, 3rd, & 4th holes together.

Notes on the C Harmonica

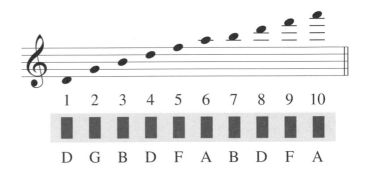

Exhaled (Blown) Notes

1	2	3	4	5	6	7	8	9	10
C	E	G	C	E	G	C	E	G	C

Inhaled (Drawn) Notes

1	2	3	4	5	6	7	8	9	10
D	G	B	D	F	A	B	D	F	A

Bends

Blow Bends

• 1/4 step

• 1/2 step

• 1 step

• 1 1/2 steps

Draw Bends

• 1/4 step

• 1/2 step

• 1 step

• 1 1/2 steps

Baby Mine

from DUMBO

Words by Ned Washington
Music by Frank Churchill

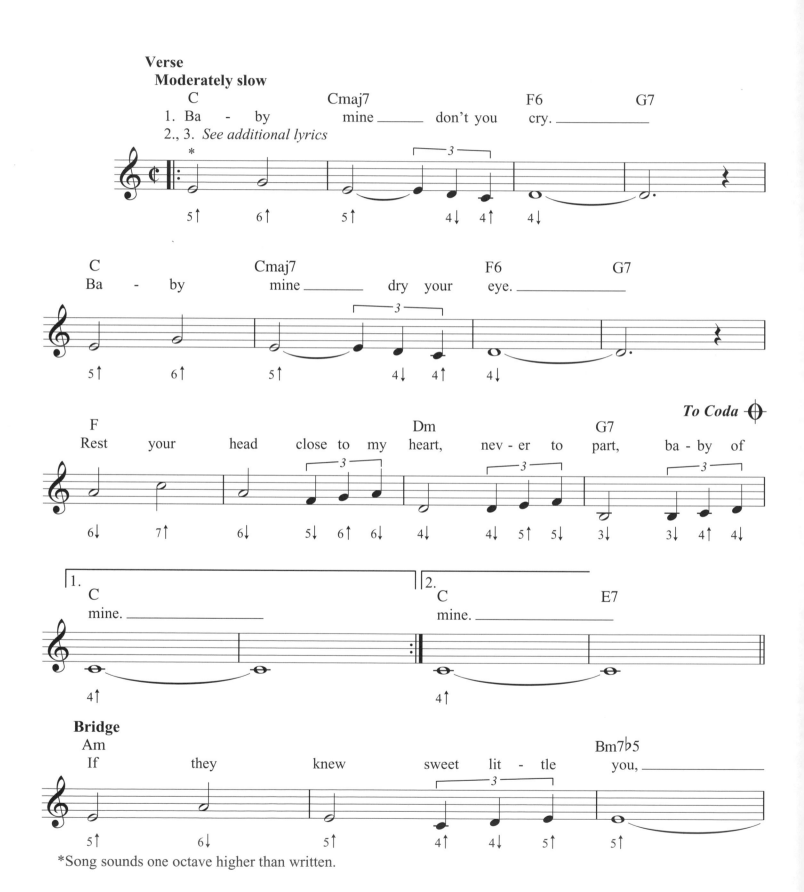

*Song sounds one octave higher than written.

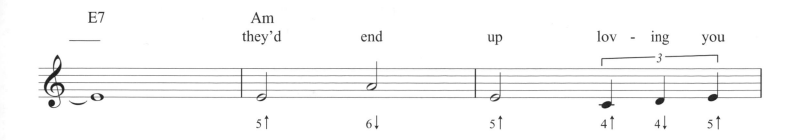

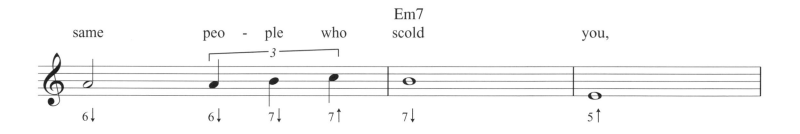

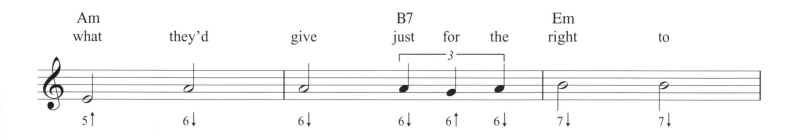

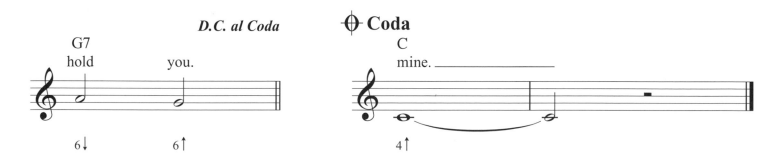

Additional Lyrics

2. Little one, when you play don't you mind what they say.
   Let those eyes sparkle and shine, never a tear, baby of mine.

3. From your head to your toes, you're not much, goodness knows,
   But you're so precious to me, sure as can be, baby of mine.

The Ballad of Davy Crockett

from DAVY CROCKETT

Words by Tom Blackburn
Music by George Bruns

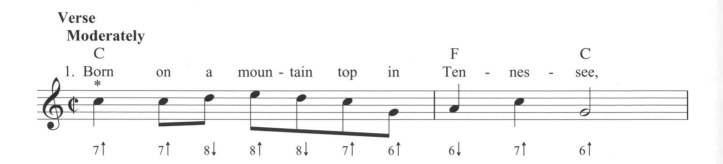

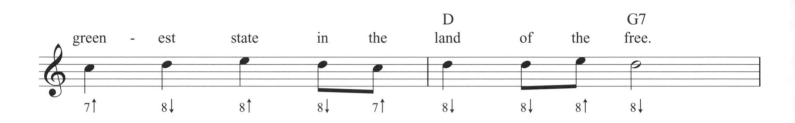

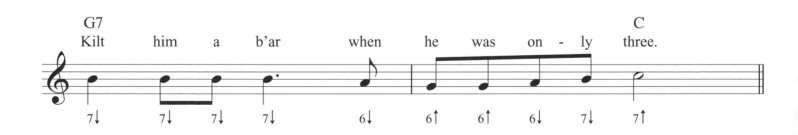

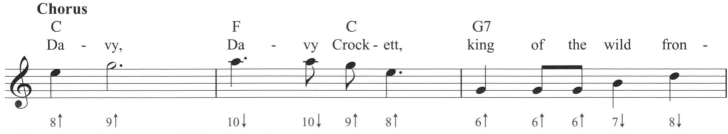

*Song sounds one octave higher than written.

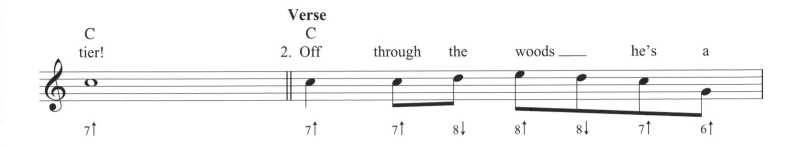

Verse

C — tier!

C — 2. Off through the woods ____ he's a

7↑ · 7↑ 7↑ 8↓ 8↑ 8↓ 7↑ 6↑

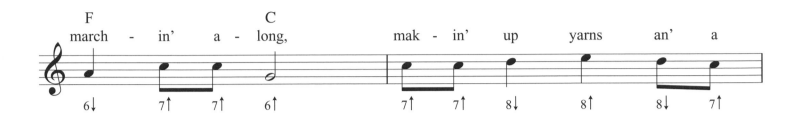

F — march - in' a - long, mak - in' up yarns an' a

6↓ 7↑ 7↑ 6↑ · 7↑ 7↑ 8↓ 8↑ 8↓ 7↑

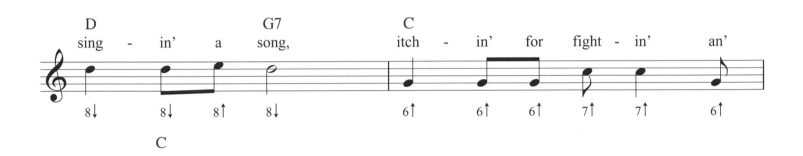

D — sing - in' a song,

G7 · C — itch - in' for fight - in' an'

8↓ 8↓ 8↑ 8↓ · 6↑ 6↑ 6↑ 7↑ 7↑ 6↑

C

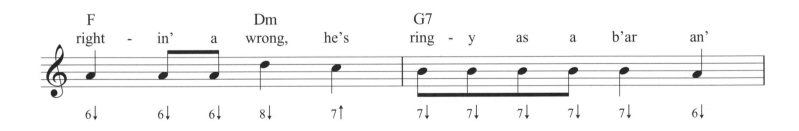

F — right - in' a

Dm — wrong, he's

G7 — ring - y as a b'ar an'

6↓ 6↓ 6↓ 8↓ 7↑ · 7↓ 7↓ 7↓ 7↓ 7↓ 6↓

Chorus

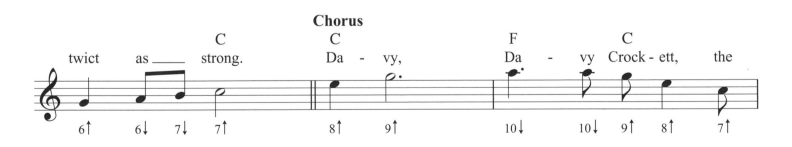

twict as ____ strong.

C — Da - vy,

C — Da - vy Crock - ett, the

F · C

6↑ 6↓ 7↓ 7↑ · 8↑ 9↑ · 10↓ 10↓ 9↑ 8↑ 7↑

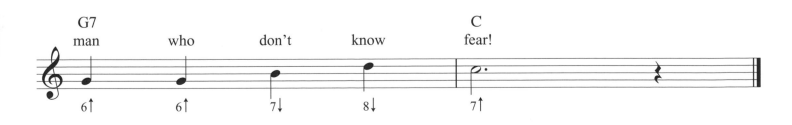

G7 — man who don't know

C — fear!

6↑ 6↑ 7↓ 8↓ · 7↑

11

The Bare Necessities

from THE JUNGLE BOOK

Words and Music by Terry Gilkyson

Chorus

With a lilt

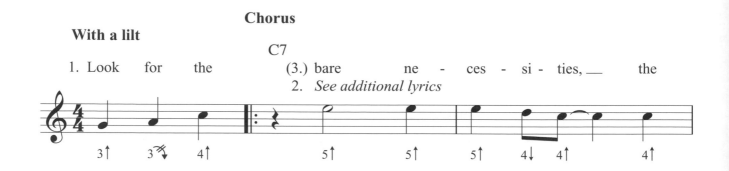

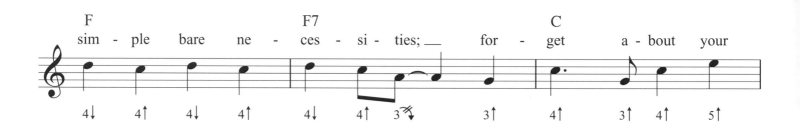

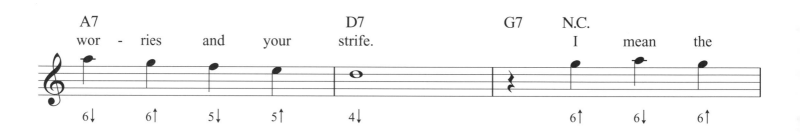

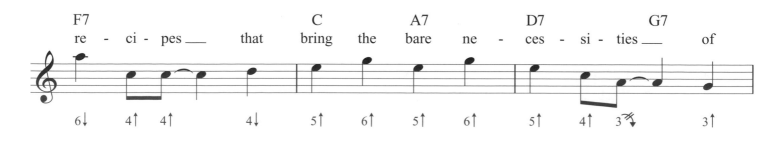

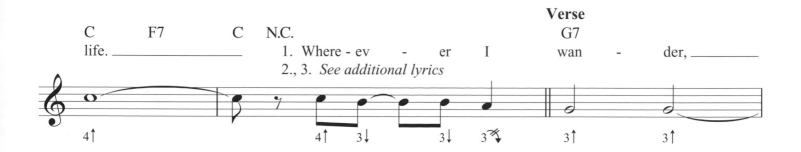

C   F7   C N.C.   G7

life. _____ 1. Where - ev - er I wan - der, _____

2., 3. *See additional lyrics*

4↑   4↑ 3↓   3↓ 3↗↓   3↑   3↑

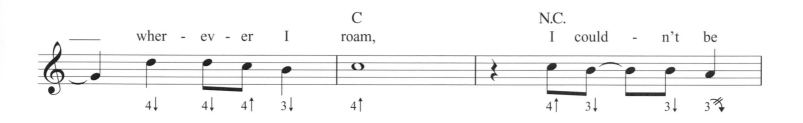

_____ wher - ev - er I roam,   I could - n't be

C   N.C.

4↓   4↓ 4↑ 3↓   4↑   4↑ 3↓   3↓ 3↗↓

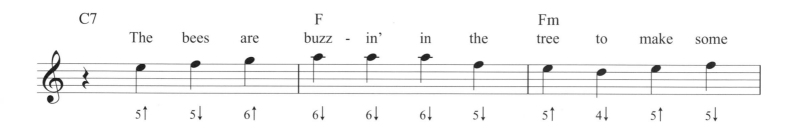

G7

fond - er _____ of my big home.

                                                  C

3↑   4↓   4↓ 4↑ 4↓ 5↑

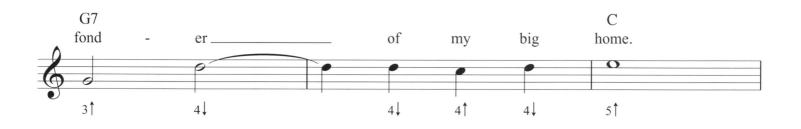

C7   F   Fm

The bees are buzz - in' in the tree to make some

5↑ 5↓ 6↑   6↓ 6↓ 6↓ 5↓   5↑ 4↓ 5↑ 5↓

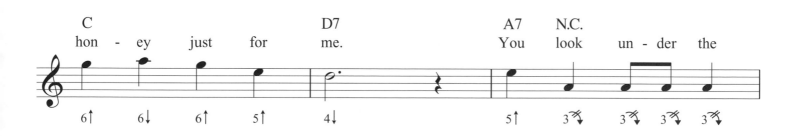

C   D7   A7 N.C.

hon - ey just for me.   You look un - der the

6↑ 6↓ 6↑ 5↑   4↓   5↑ 3↗↓ 3↗↓ 3↗↓ 3↗↓

A7   N.C.   Dm   N.C.

rock and plants and take a glance at the

5↑ 3↗↓ 3↗↓ 3↗↓   5↓ 5↓ 5↓   5↑ 5↑

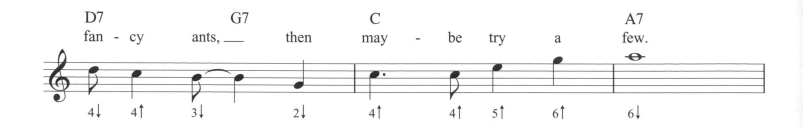

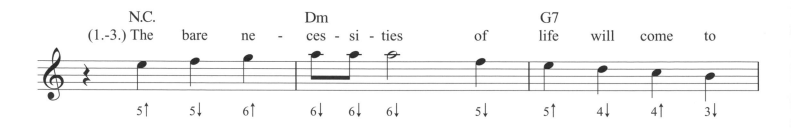

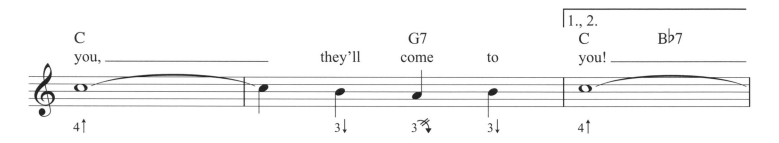

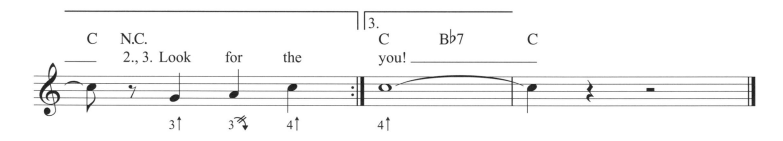

Additional Lyrics

Chorus 2. Bare necessities, the simple bare necessities;
Forget about your worries and your strife.
I mean the bare necessities,
That's why a bear can rest at ease
With just the bare necessities of life.

Verse 2. When you pick a pawpaw or a prickly pear,
And you prick a raw paw, next time beware.
Don't pick the prickly pear by paw,
When you pick a pear, try to use the claw.
But you don't need to use the claw
When you pick a pear of the big pawpaw,
Have I given you a clue?

Verse 3. So just try to relax *(spoken: Oh yeah!)* in my backyard.
If you act like that bee acts, you're workin' too hard.
Don't spend your time just lookin' around
For something you want that can't be found.
When you find out you can live without it
And go along not thinkin' about it,
I'll tell you something true.

Can You Feel the Love Tonight

from THE LION KING

Music by Elton John
Lyrics by Tim Rice

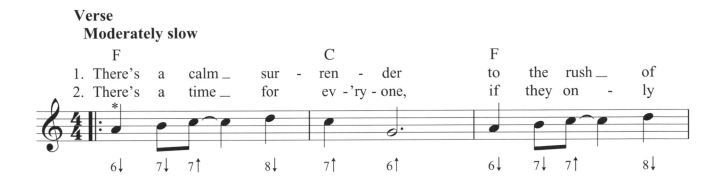

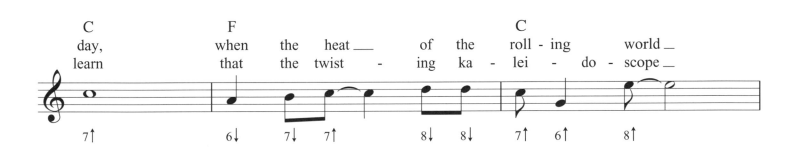

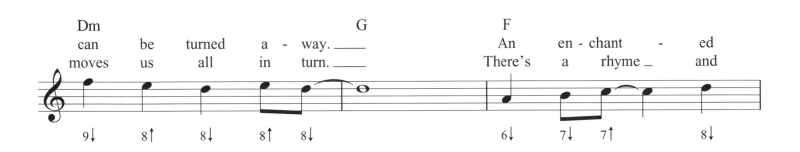

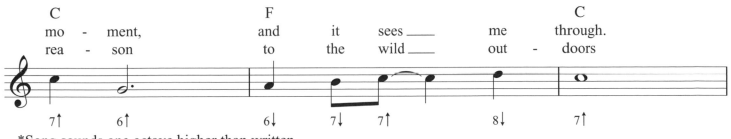

*Song sounds one octave higher than written.

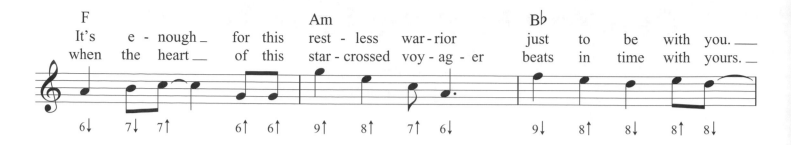

Chorus

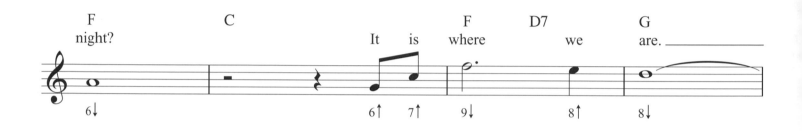

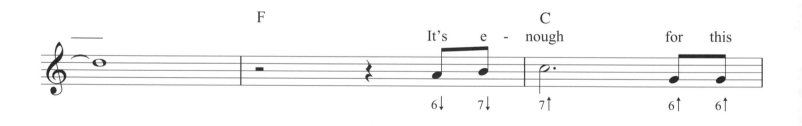

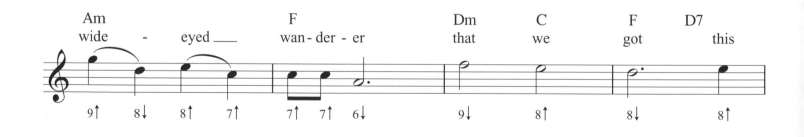

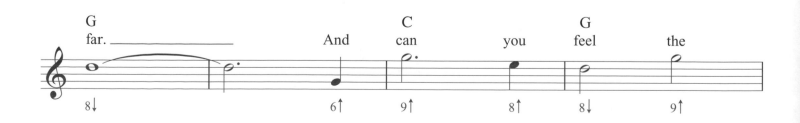

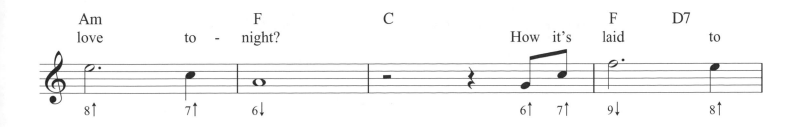

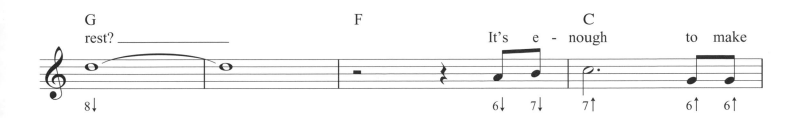

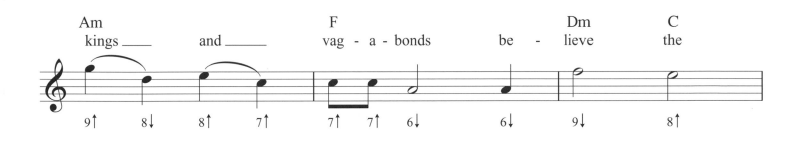

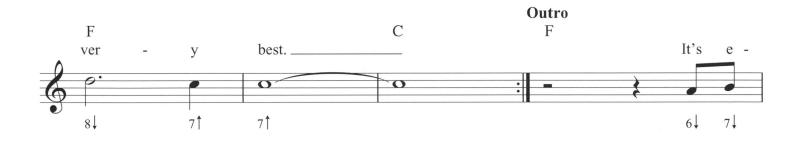

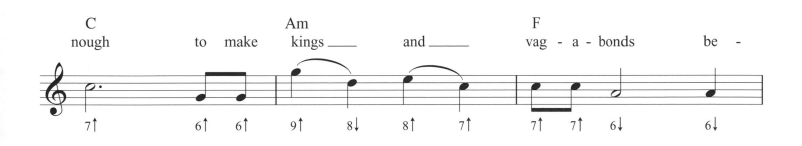

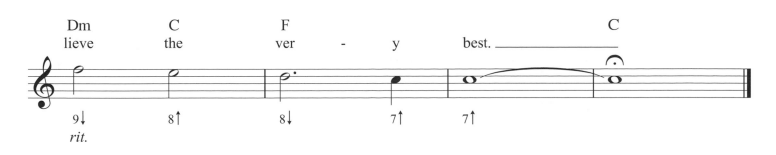

Beauty and the Beast

from BEAUTY AND THE BEAST

Music by Alan Menken
Lyrics by Howard Ashman

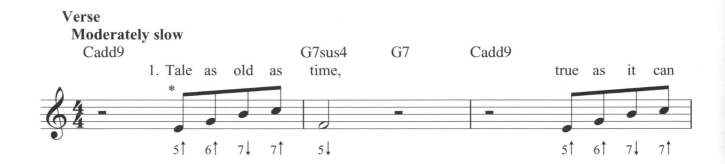

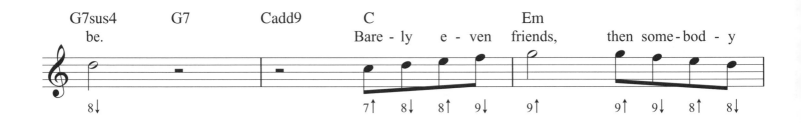

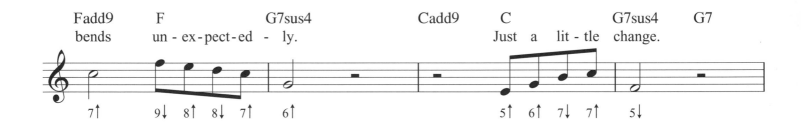

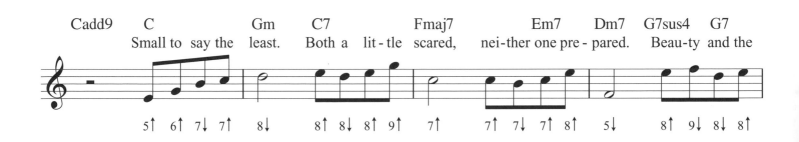

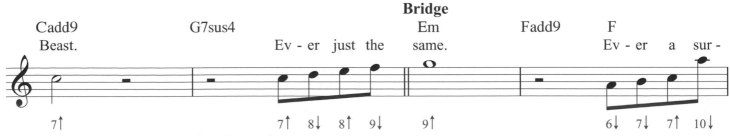

*Song sounds one octave higher than written.

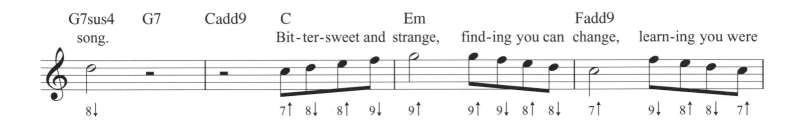

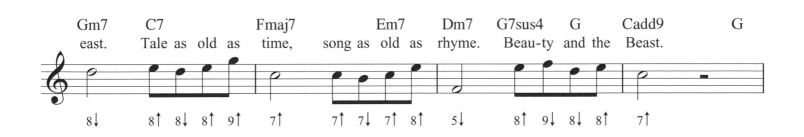

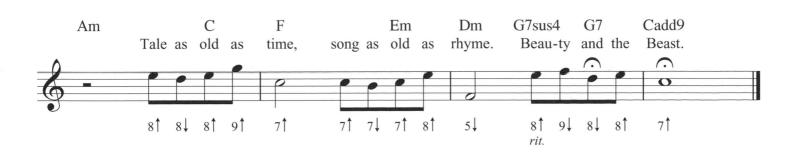

Bibbidi-Bobbidi-Boo
(The Magic Song)

from CINDERELLA

Words by Jerry Livingston
Music by Mack David and Al Hoffman

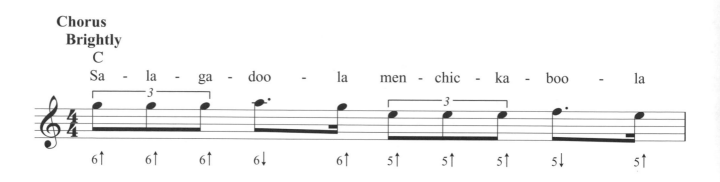

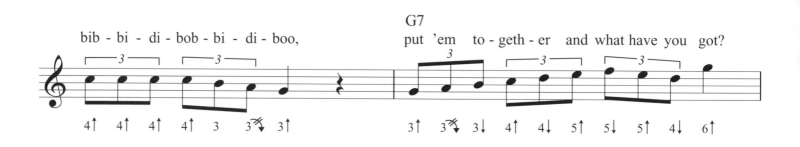

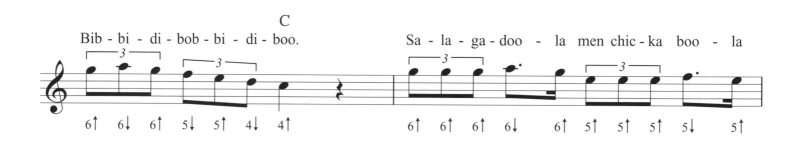

Bridge

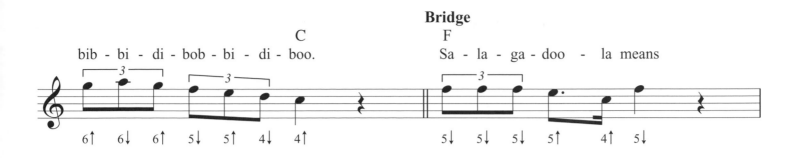

C
bib - bi - di - bob - bi - di - boo.

F
Sa - la - ga - doo - la means

6↑ 6↓ 6↑ 5↓ 5↑ 4↓ 4↑   5↓ 5↓ 5↓ 5↑ 4↑ 5↓

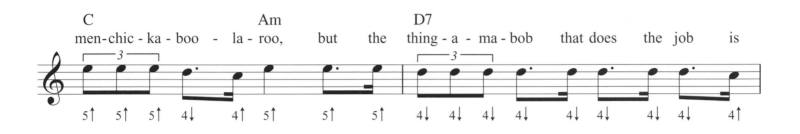

C
men - chic - ka - boo - la - roo,

Am
but   the

D7
thing - a - ma - bob   that does   the job   is

5↑ 5↑ 5↑ 4↓ 4↑ 5↑   5↑ 5↑   4↓ 4↓ 4↓ 4↓ 4↓ 4↓ 4↓ 4↓ 4↑

Chorus

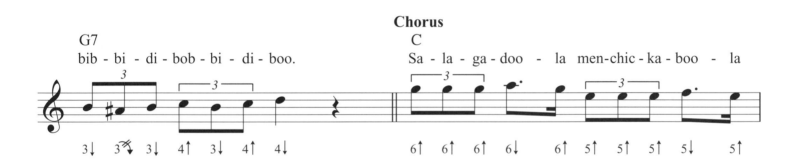

G7
bib - bi - di - bob - bi - di - boo.

C
Sa - la - ga - doo - la men - chic - ka - boo - la

3↓ 3↗↙ 3↓ 4↑ 3↓ 4↑ 4↓   6↑ 6↑ 6↑ 6↓ 6↑ 5↑ 5↑ 5↑ 5↓ 5↑

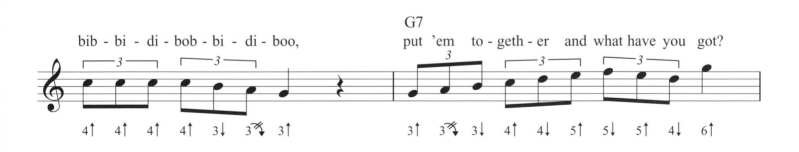

bib - bi - di - bob - bi - di - boo,

G7
put 'em to - geth - er   and what have you got?

4↑ 4↑ 4↑ 4↑ 3↓ 3↗↙ 3↑   3↑ 3↗↙ 3↓ 4↑ 4↓ 5↑ 5↓ 5↑ 4↓ 6↑

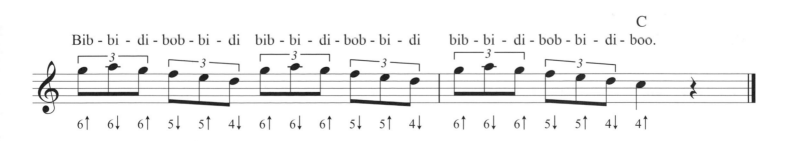

C
Bib - bi - di - bob - bi - di bib - bi - di - bob - bi - di bib - bi - di - bob - bi - di - boo.

6↑ 6↓ 6↑ 5↓ 5↑ 4↓ 6↑ 6↓ 6↑ 5↓ 5↑ 4↓ 6↑ 6↓ 6↑ 5↓ 5↑ 4↓ 4↑

Candle on the Water

from PETE'S DRAGON

Words and Music by Al Kasha and Joel Hirschhorn

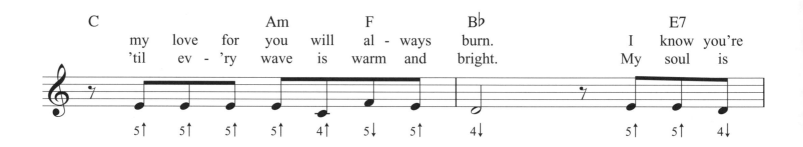

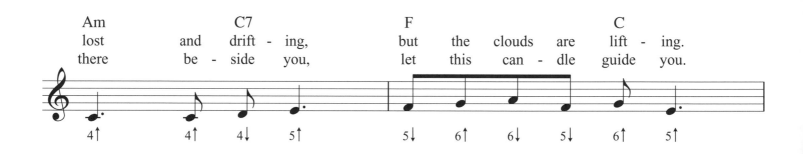

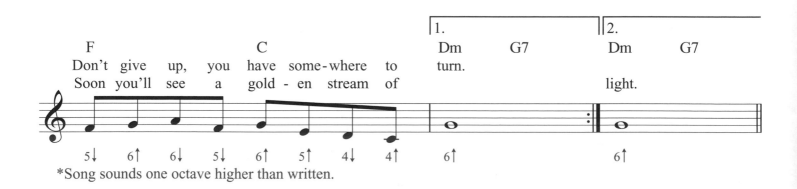

*Song sounds one octave higher than written.

Bridge

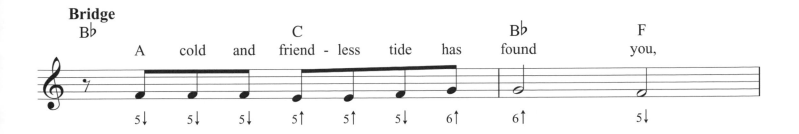

Bb   C   Bb   F

A cold and friend - less tide has found you,

5↓ 5↓ 5↓ 5↑ 5↑ 5↓ 6↑   6↑   5↓

Bb   C   F

don't let the storm - y dark - ness pull you down.

5↓ 5↓ 5↓ 5↑ 5↑ 5↓ 6↑   6↓ 6↑ 5↓

Am7   D7   Am7   G

I'll paint a ray of hope a - round you,

6↑ 6↑ 6↑ 6↓ 6↑ 6↑ 6↓ 6↓ 6↑

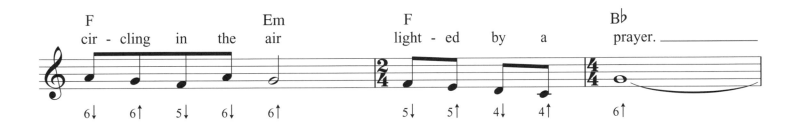

F   Em   F   Bb

cir - cling in the air light - ed by a prayer. _____

6↓ 6↑ 5↓ 6↓ 6↑   5↓ 5↑ 4↓ 4↑   6↑

Verse

G7   C   Dm   F   G

3. I'll be your can - dle on the wa - ter,

4↑ 4↑ 4↑ 4↓ 5↑ 5↓ 4↓ 6↓ 6↑

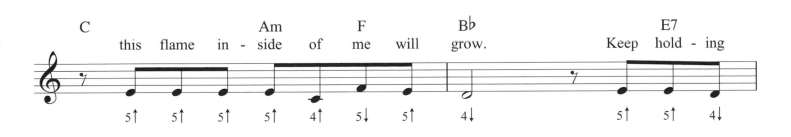

C   Am   F   Bb   E7

this flame in - side of me will grow. Keep hold - ing

5↑ 5↑ 5↑ 5↑ 4↑ 5↓ 5↑ 4↓   5↑ 5↑ 4↓

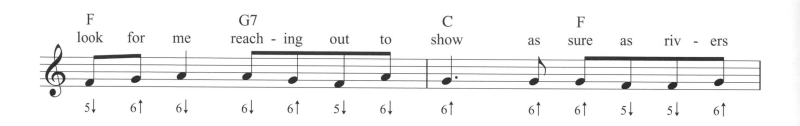

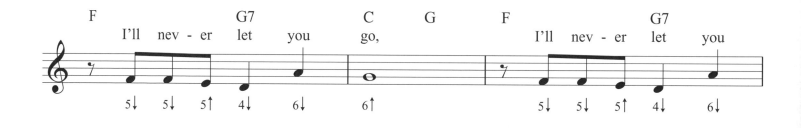

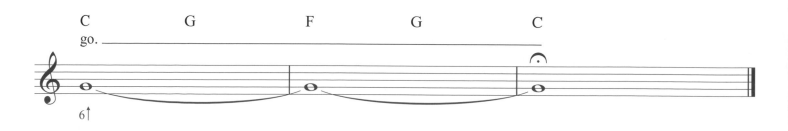

Colors of the Wind

from POCAHONTAS

Music by Alan Menken
Lyrics by Stephen Schwartz

Am　　　　　　　　　　　　　　　　　　　　Em
asked　the　grin - ning　bob - cat　why　he　grinned?　　　　　Can　you

7↑　7↓　7↓　6↓　6↓　6↑　6↑　5↑　6↑　　　　5↑　6↑

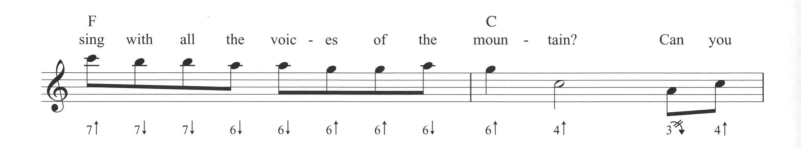

F　　　　　　　　　　　　　　　　　　　C
sing　with　all　the　voic - es　of　the　moun - tain?　　　　Can　you

7↑　7↓　7↓　6↓　6↓　6↑　6↑　6↓　6↑　4↑　3↓　4↑

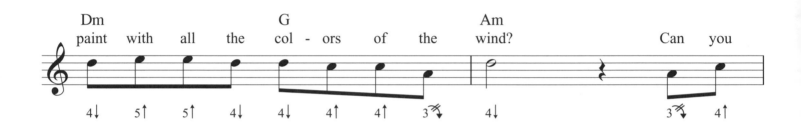

Dm　　　　　　　　　G　　　　　　　　　Am
paint　with　all　the　col - ors　of　the　wind?　　　　Can　you

4↓　5↑　5↑　4↓　4↓　4↑　4↑　3↓　4↓　　　3↓　4↑

D.S. al Coda
(take repeat)

F　　　　　　　　G7　　　　　　　　C
paint　with　all　the　col - ors　of　the　wind? _____　　　3. Come

4↓　5↑　5↑　4↓　4↓　4↑　3↓　4↑　4↑　　　　　　3↑

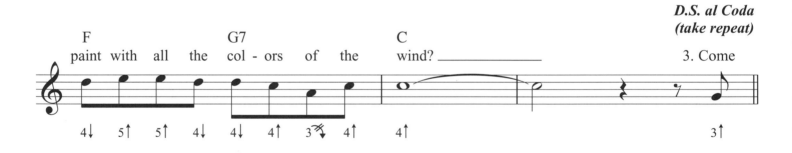

⊕ **Coda**　　　　　　　**Bridge**
C　　　　　　　　Em　　　F　　　　Em　　Am
ends.　　　　How　high　does　the　syc - a - more　grow?　If　you

4↑　　　　　6↑　7↓　6↓　6↑　6↑　6↓　6↑　4↑　3↓　4↑

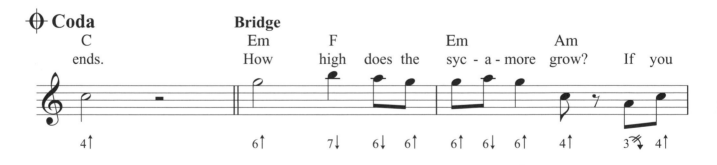

F　　　　　　　　　　　G7
cut　it　down　　then　you'll　nev - er　know.　　　　　And　you'll

4↓　5↑　4↓　　4↑　4↓　5↑　4↓　4↓　　　　　6↓　7↓

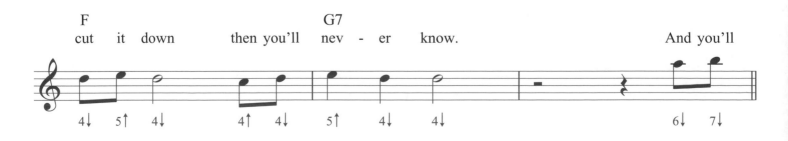

Chorus

Additional Lyrics

2. You think the only people who are people
   Are the people who look and think like you,
   But if you walk the footsteps of a stranger
   You'll learn things you never knew you never knew.

3. Come run the hidden pine trails of the forest,
   Come taste the sunsweet berries of the earth,
   Come roll in all the riches all around you
   And for once, never wonder what they're worth.

4. The rainstorm and the rivers are my brothers;
   The heron and the otter are my friends;
   And we are all connected to each other
   In a circle, in a hoop that never ends.

Circle of Life

from THE LION KING

Music by Elton John
Lyrics by Tim Rice

Verse 𝄋
Relaxed Pop beat

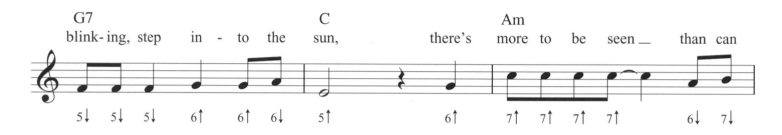

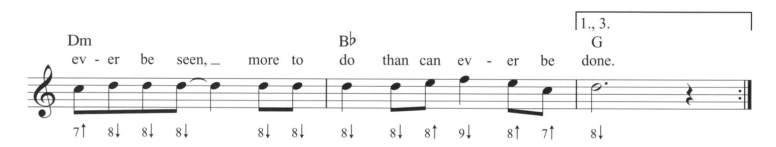

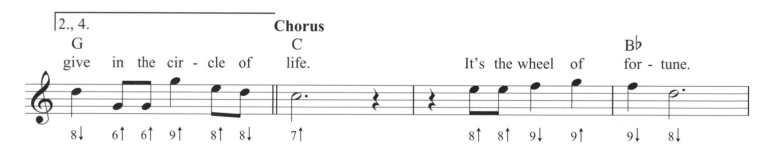

*Song sounds one octave higher than written.

To Coda

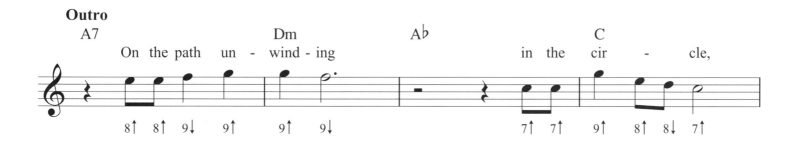

⊕ Coda

D.S. al Coda
(take repeat)

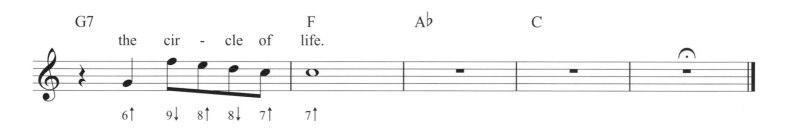

Outro

Additional Lyrics

2. Some say, "Eat or be eaten."
   Some say, "Live and let live."
   But all are agreed as they join the stampede,
   You should never take more than you give…

3. Some of us fall by the wayside,
   And some of us soar to the stars.
   And some of us sail through our troubles,
   And some have to live with the scars.

4. There's far too much to take in here,
   More to find than can ever be found.
   But the sun rolling high in the sapphire sky
   Keeps great and small on the endless round…

Do You Want to Build a Snowman?

from FROZEN

Music and Lyrics by Kristen Anderson-Lopez and Robert Lopez

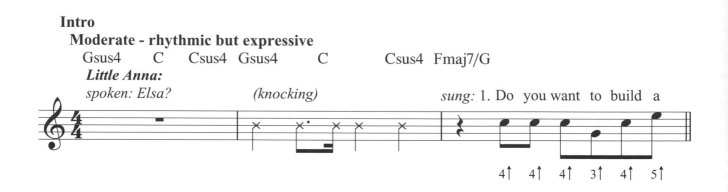

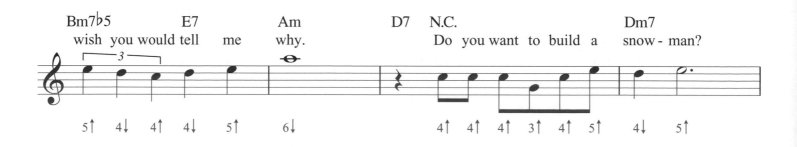

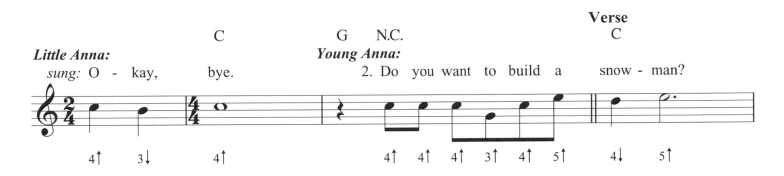

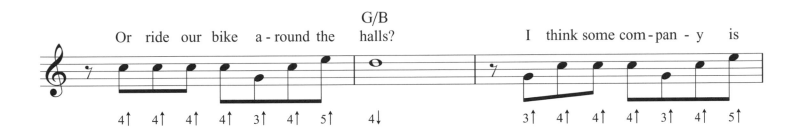

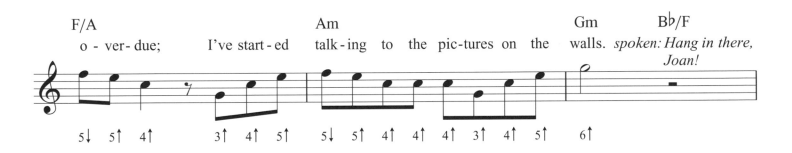

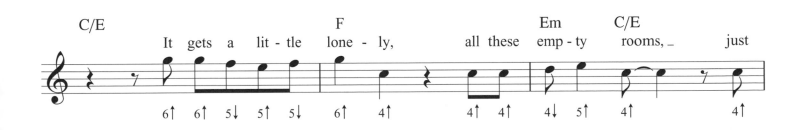

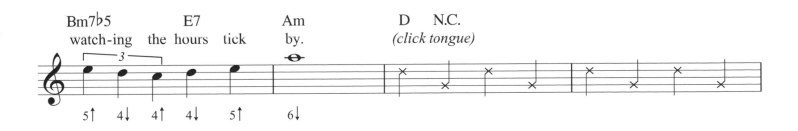

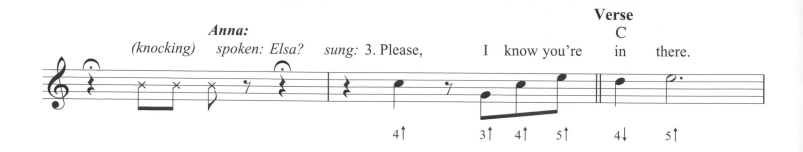

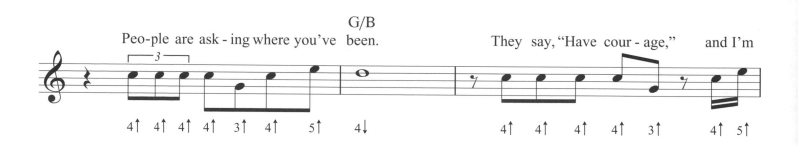

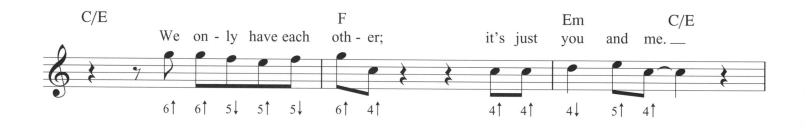

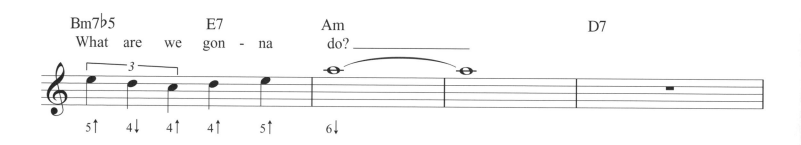

Heigh-Ho

The Dwarfs' Marching Song from
SNOW WHITE AND THE SEVEN DWARFS
Words by Larry Morey
Music by Frank Churchill

*Song sounds one octave higher than written.

I See the Light

from TANGLED

Music by Alan Menken
Lyrics by Glenn Slater

Verse
Moderately slow

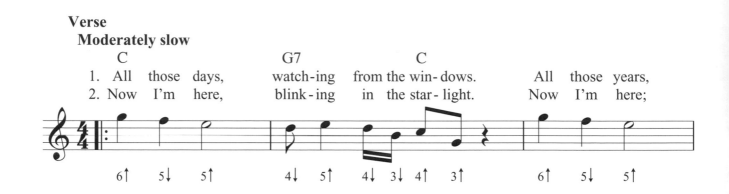

1. All those days, watch-ing from the win-dows. All those years,
2. Now I'm here, blink-ing in the star-light. Now I'm here;

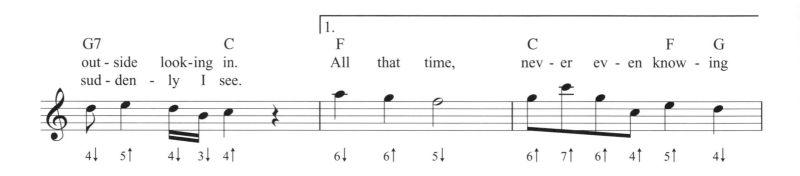

1. out-side look-ing in. All that time, nev-er ev-en know-ing
2. sud-den-ly I see.

1. All that time, nev-er ev-en know-ing

just how blind I've been.

2. Stand-ing here, it's

oh, so clear I'm where I'm meant to be. And at

Chorus

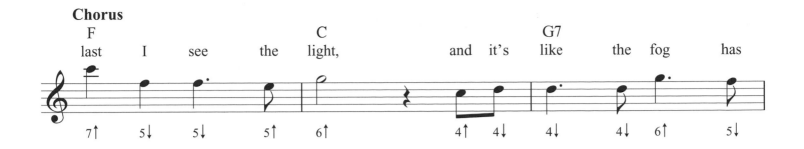

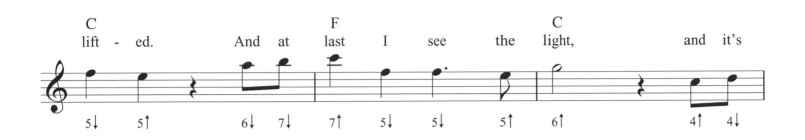

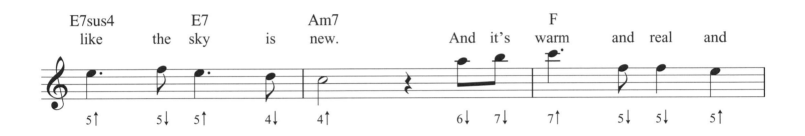

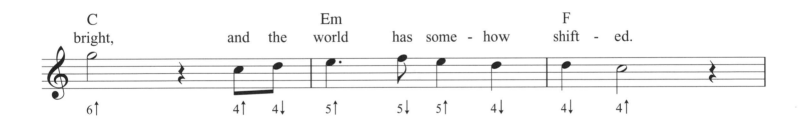

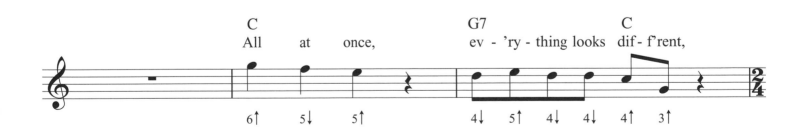

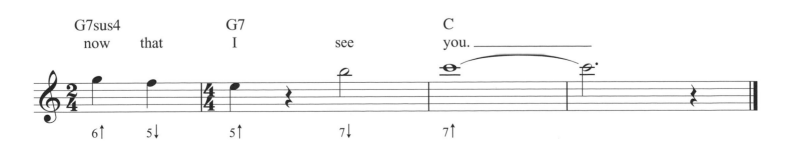

I'm Late

from ALICE IN WONDERLAND

Words by Bob Hilliard
Music by Sammy Fain

Verse
Moderately fast

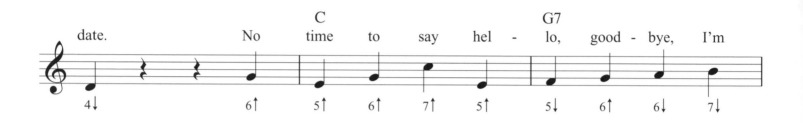

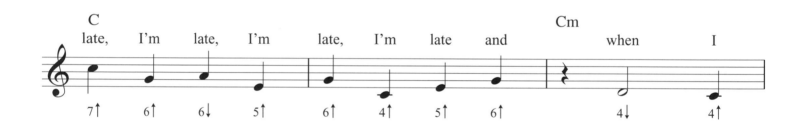

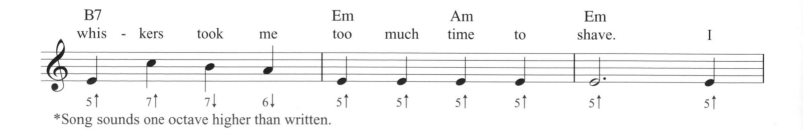

*Song sounds one octave higher than written.

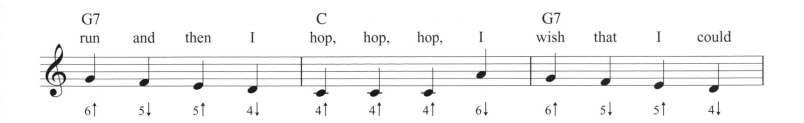

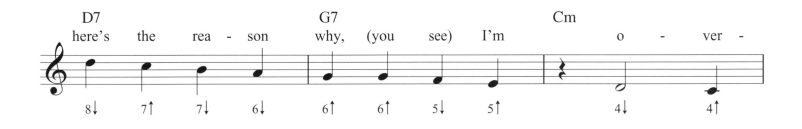

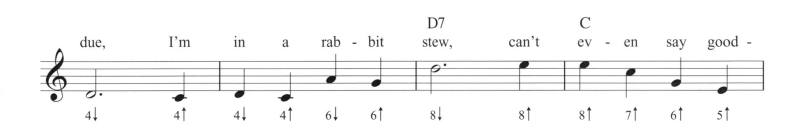

I'm Wishing

from SNOW WHITE AND THE SEVEN DWARFS

Words by Larry Morey
Music by Frank Churchill

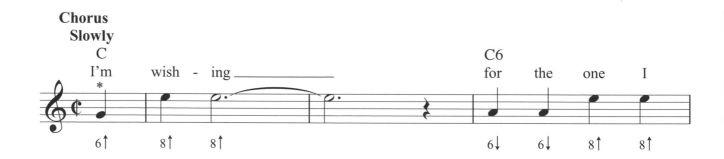

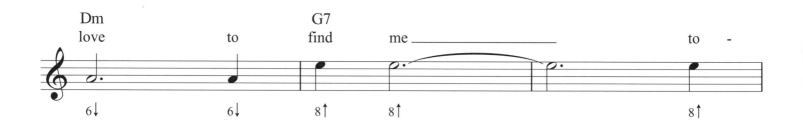

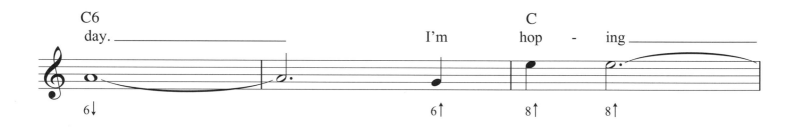

*Song sounds one octave higher than written.

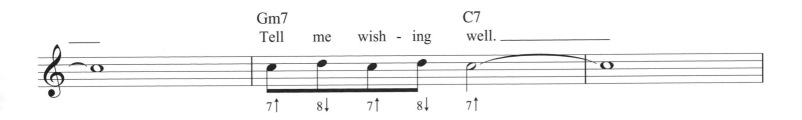

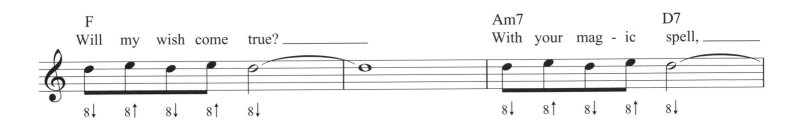

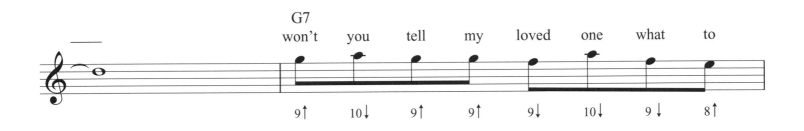

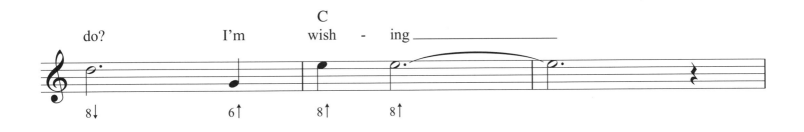

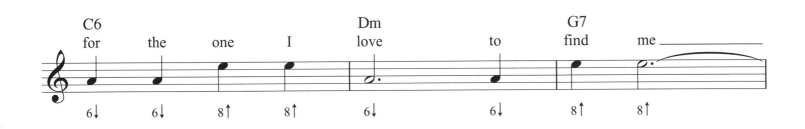

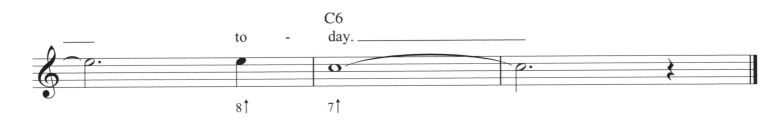

I've Got No Strings

from PINOCCHIO

Words by Ned Washington
Music by Leigh Harline

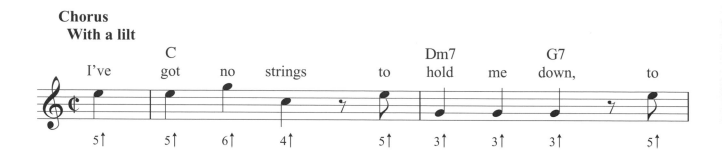

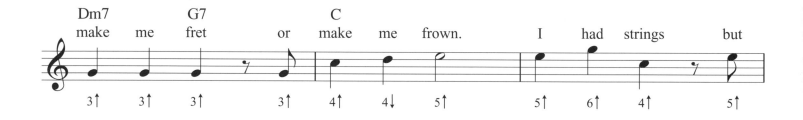

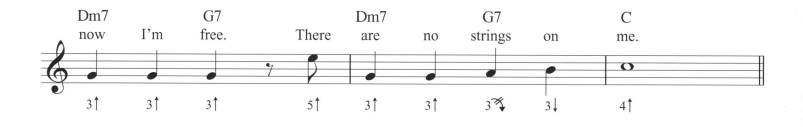

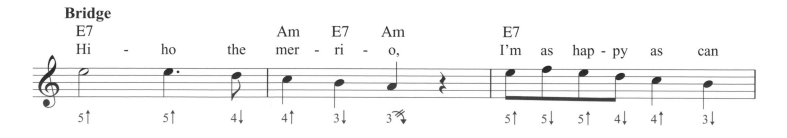

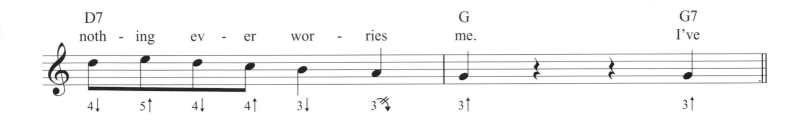

Chorus

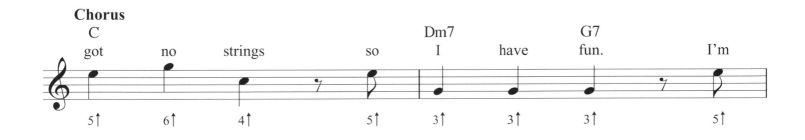

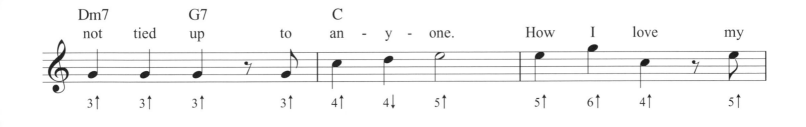

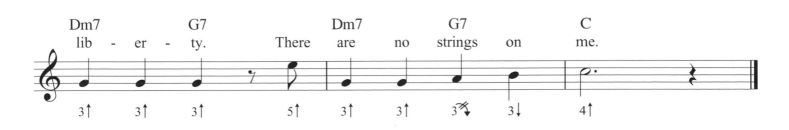

It's a Small World

from Disneyland Resort® and Magic Kingdom® Park

Words and Music by Richard M. Sherman and Robert B. Sherman

Verse
March

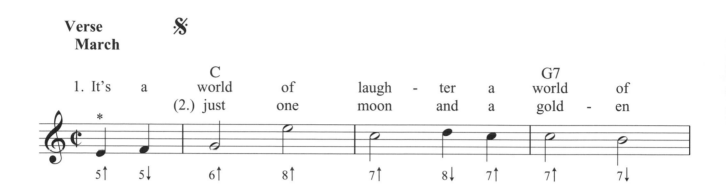

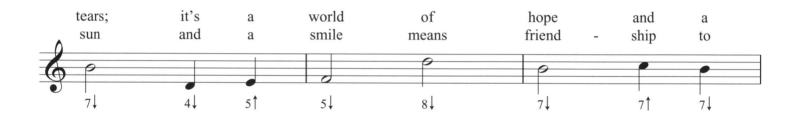

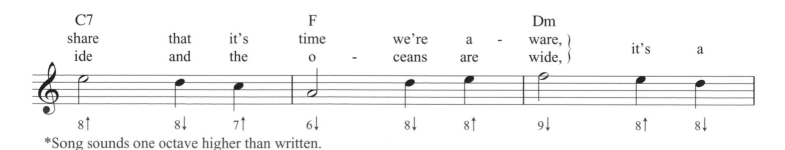

*Song sounds one octave higher than written.

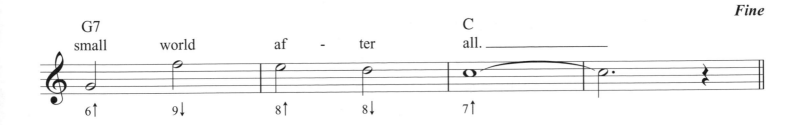

Chorus

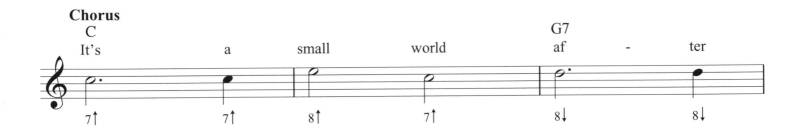

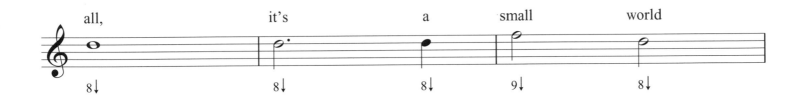

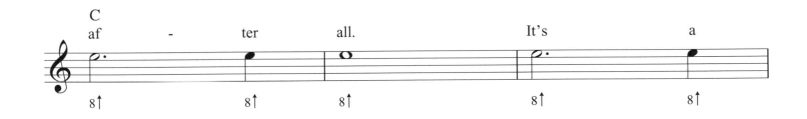

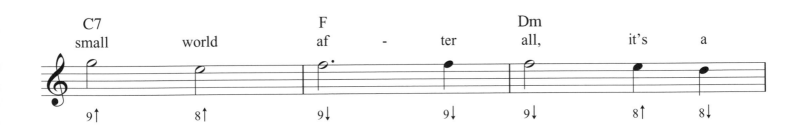

D.S. al Fine

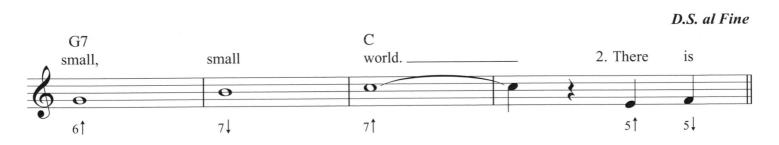

Lavender Blue
(Dilly Dilly)
from SO DEAR TO MY HEART

Words by Larry Morey
Music by Eliot Daniel

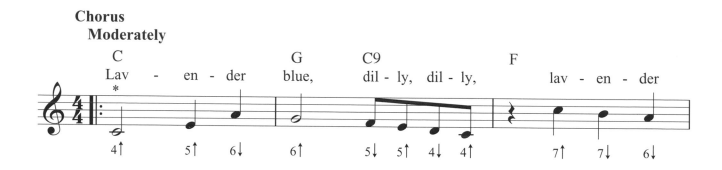

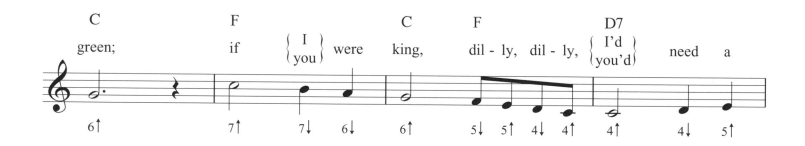

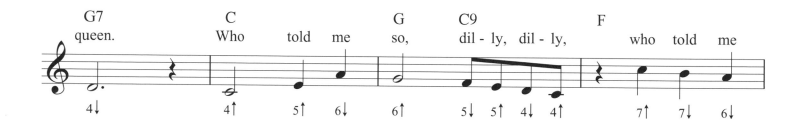

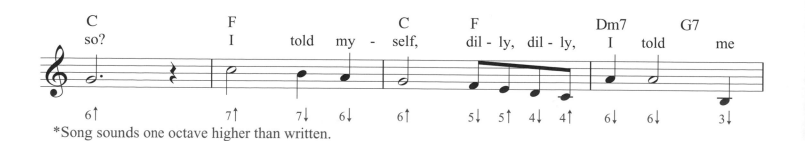

*Song sounds one octave higher than written.

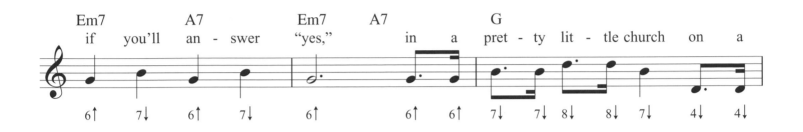

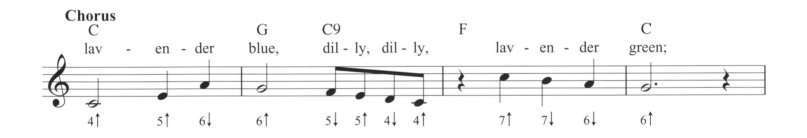

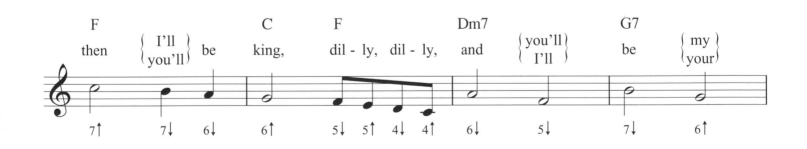

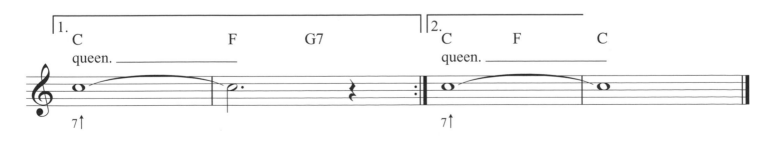

Mickey Mouse March

from THE MICKEY MOUSE CLUB

Words and Music by Jimmie Dodd

Intro
Brightly

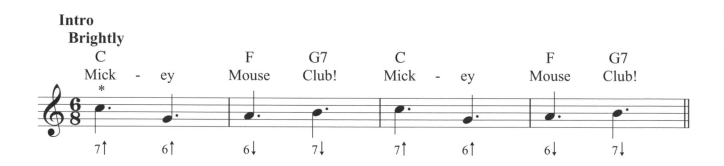

Verse

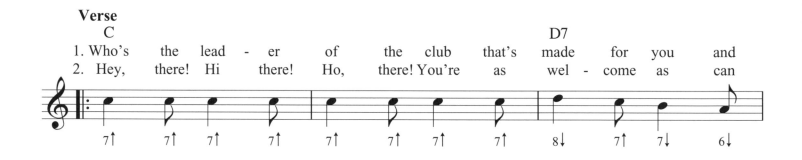

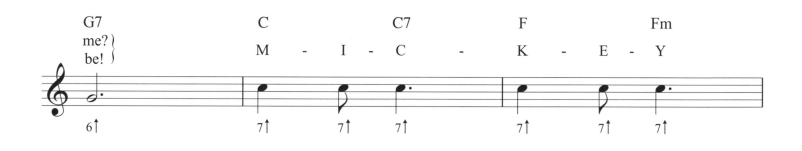

*Song sounds one octave higher than written.

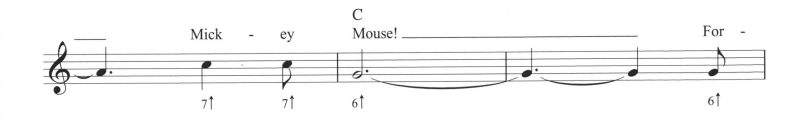

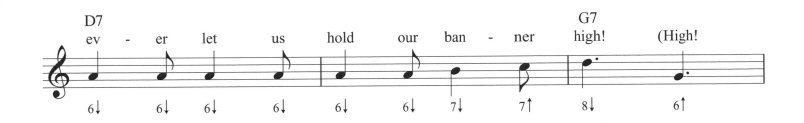

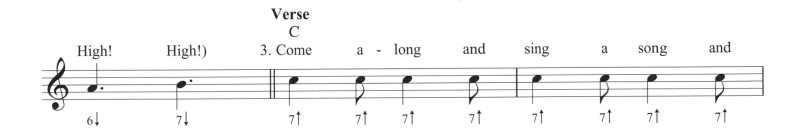

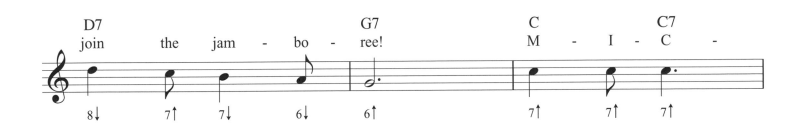

Never Smile at a Crocodile

from PETER PAN

Words by Jack Lawrence
Music by Frank Churchill

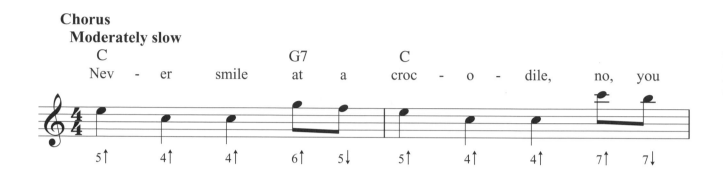

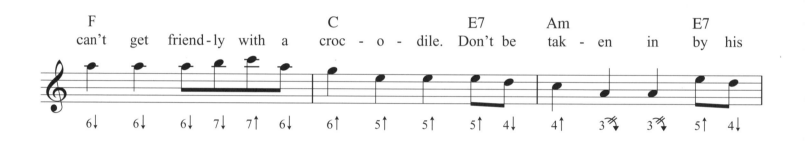

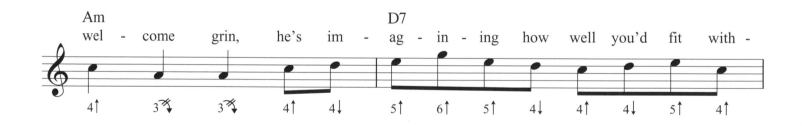

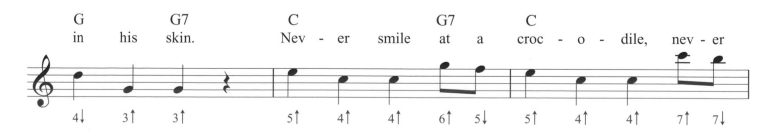

F   C   F   C

tip your hat and stop to talk a while. { Nev - er run, walk a - way, say "Good-
                   Don't be rude, nev - er mock, throw a

6↓ 6↓ 6↓ 7↓ 7↑ 6↓ 6↑ 5↑ 5↑ 7↑ 7↓ 6↓ 7↑ 6↓ 6↑ 7↑ 7↓

To Coda ⊕

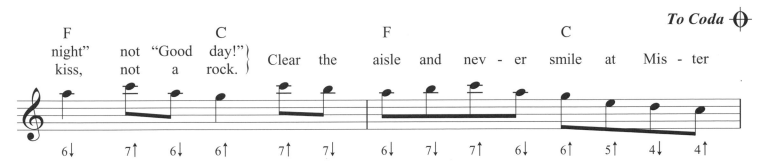

F   C   F   C

night" not "Good day!") Clear the aisle and nev - er smile at Mis - ter
kiss, not a rock. }

6↓ 7↑ 6↓ 6↑ 7↑ 7↓ 6↓ 7↓ 7↑ 6↓ 6↑ 5↑ 4↓ 4↑

Bridge

     G7 C   F   C7

Croc - o - dile. You may ver - y well be well - bred,

5↑ 4↓ 4↑   4↑ 5↓ 5↓ 5↓ 5↑ 4↓ 4↑ 4↓

F   C7   F

lots of et - i - quette in your head, but there's al - ways

4↑ 5↓ 5↓ 5↓ 5↑ 4↓ 4↑ 4↓ 4↑ 6↓ 6↓ 6↓

C   F   C   G7

some spe - cial case, time or place, to for - get et - i -

6↑ 6↓ 6↑ 5↓ 6↑ 5↓ 5↑ 5↓ 5↑ 4↓ 5↑ 4↓

⊕ **Coda**

D.C. al Coda

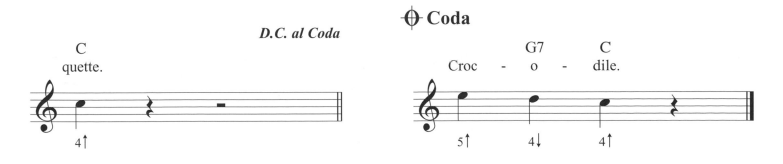

C   G7   C

quette.   Croc - o - dile.

4↑   5↑ 4↓ 4↑

Part of Your World

from THE LITTLE MERMAID

Music by Alan Menken
Lyrics by Howard Ashman

Verse
Moderately bright

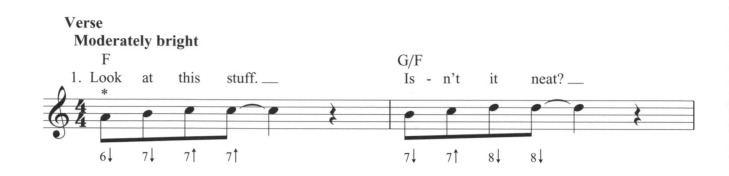

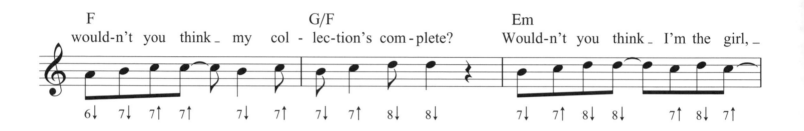

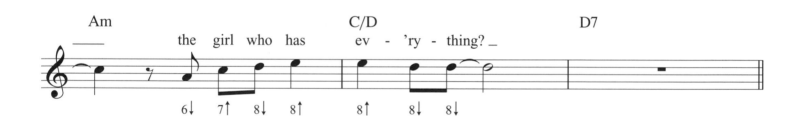

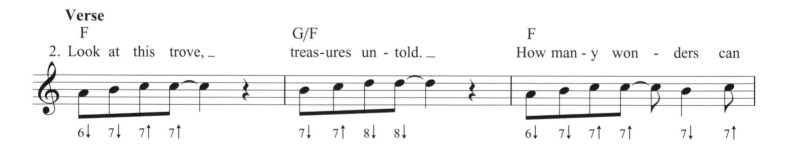

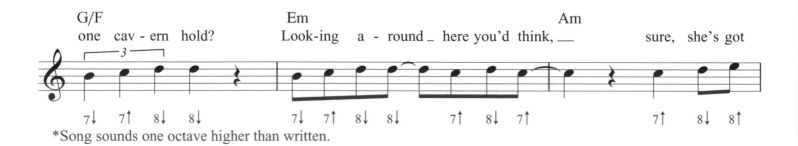

*Song sounds one octave higher than written.

Pre-Chorus

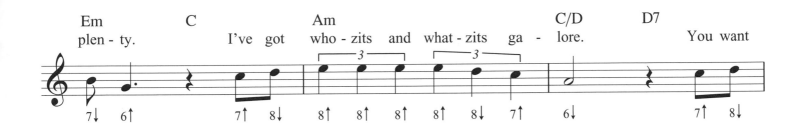

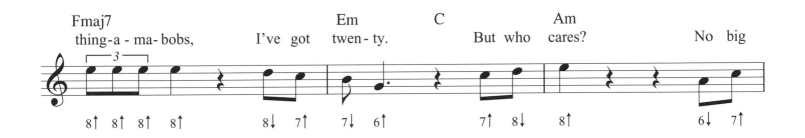

Chorus

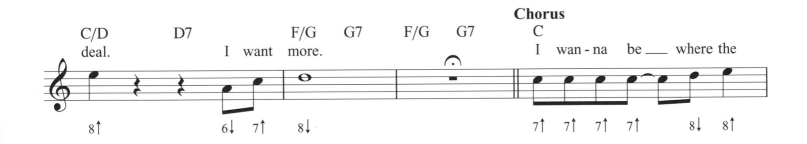

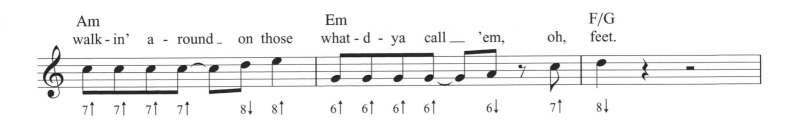

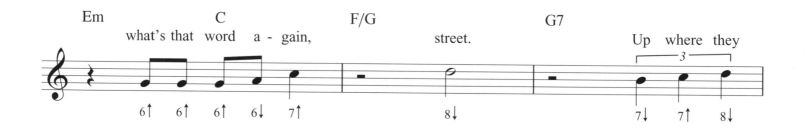

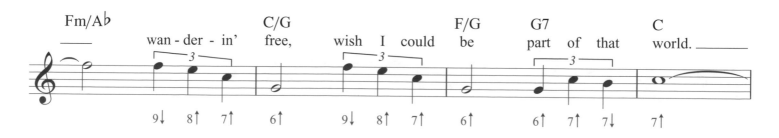

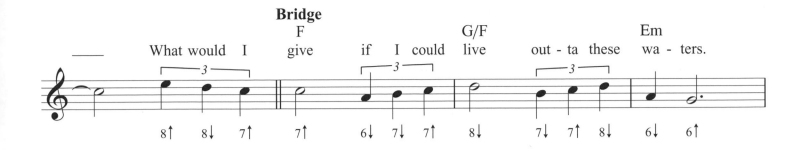

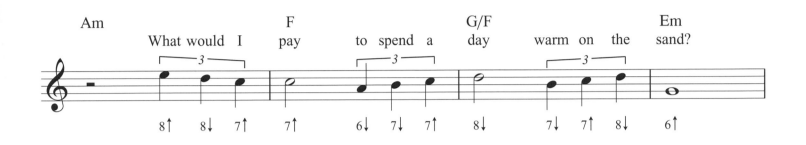

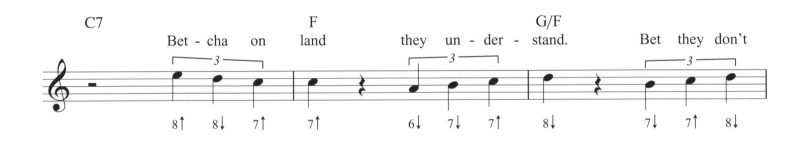

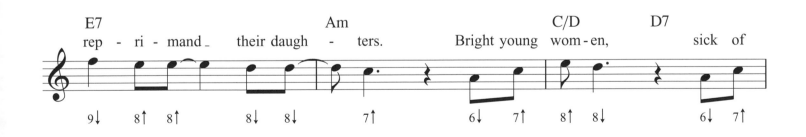

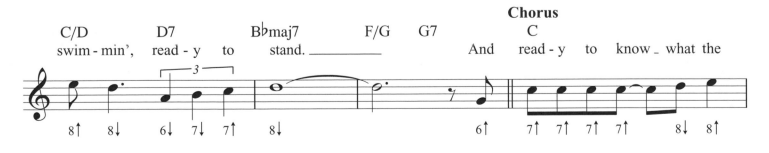

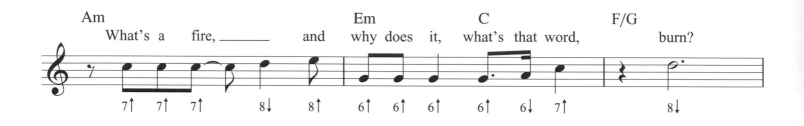

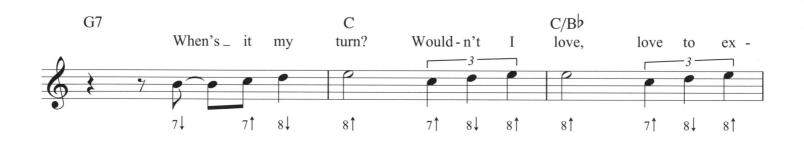

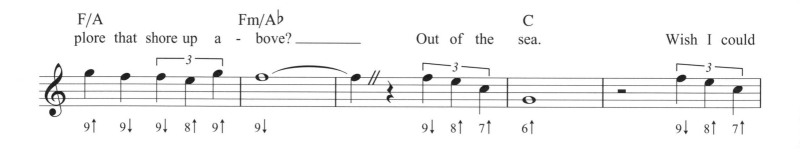

Supercalifragilisticexpialidocious

from MARY POPPINS

Words and Music by Richard M. Sherman and Robert B. Sherman

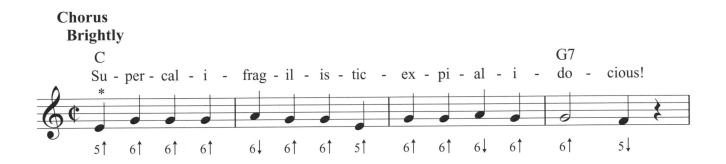

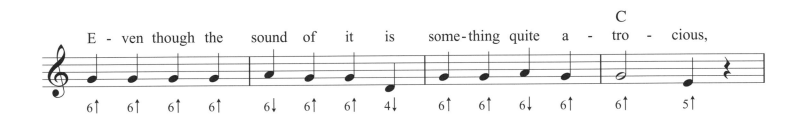

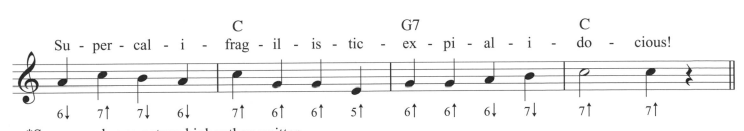

*Song sounds one octave higher than written.

Bridge

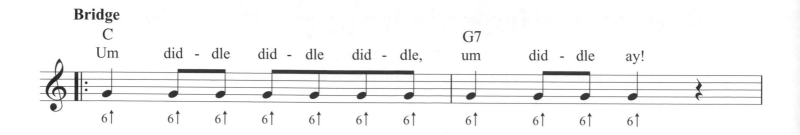

C

Um did - dle did - dle did - dle, um did - dle ay!

G7

C

Um did - dle did - dle did - dle, um did - dle ay! 1. Be -

G7

Verse

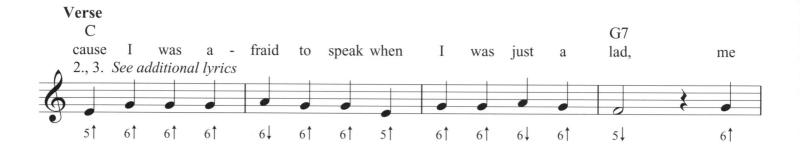

C

cause I was a - fraid to speak when I was just a lad, me
2., 3. *See additional lyrics*

G7

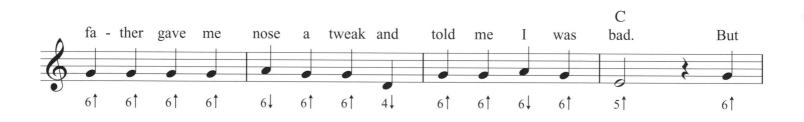

fa - ther gave me nose a tweak and told me I was bad. But

C

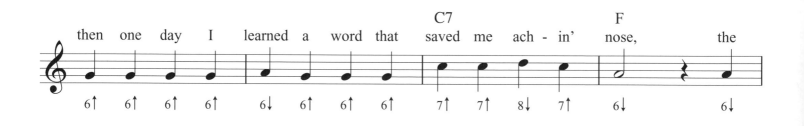

then one day I learned a word that saved me ach - in' nose, the

C7   F

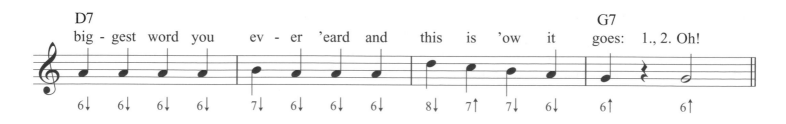

big - gest word you ev - er 'eard and this is 'ow it goes: 1., 2. Oh!

D7   G7

56

Chorus

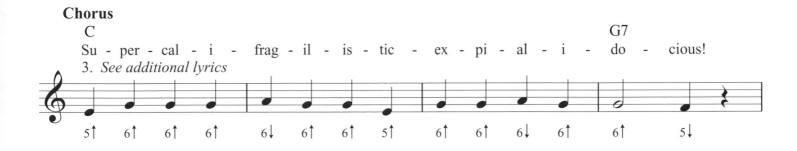

C   G7

Su - per - cal - i - frag - il - is - tic - ex - pi - al - i - do - cious!

3. *See additional lyrics*

5↑ 6↑ 6↑ 6↑ 6↓ 6↑ 6↑ 5↑ 6↑ 6↑ 6↓ 6↑ 6↑ 5↓

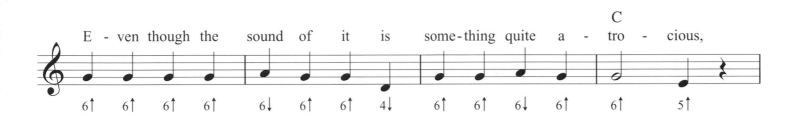

                                                        C

E - ven though the sound of it is some-thing quite a - tro - cious,

6↑ 6↑ 6↑ 6↑ 6↓ 6↑ 6↑ 4↓ 6↑ 6↑ 6↓ 6↑ 6↑ 5↑

                                     C7   F

if you say it loud e - nough you'll al - ways sound pre - co - cious.

6↑ 6↑ 6↑ 6↑ 6↓ 6↑ 6↑ 6↑ 7↑ 7↑ 8↓ 7↑ 7↑ 6↓

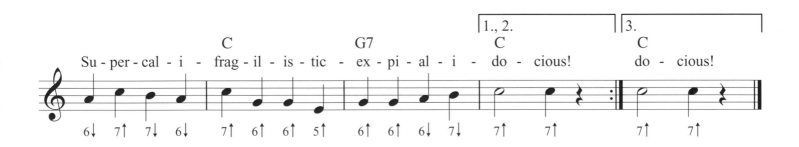

                   C   G7   1., 2.   3.
                                                              C   C

Su - per - cal - i - frag - il - is - tic - ex - pi - al - i - do - cious!   do - cious!

6↓ 7↑ 7↓ 6↓ 7↑ 6↑ 6↑ 5↑ 6↑ 6↑ 6↓ 7↓ 7↑ 7↑   7↑ 7↑

Additional Lyrics

2. He traveled all around the world and everywhere he went
He'd use his word and all would say, "There goes a clever gent!"
When dukes and ma'arajas pass the time of day with me,
I say me special word and then they ask me out to tea. Oh!

3. So when the cat has got your tongue, there's no need for dismay.
Just summon up this word and then you're got a lot to say.
But better use it carefully or it can change your life.
One hight I said it to me girl and now me girl's me wife.

Chorus 3. She's supercalifragilisticexpialidocious!
Supercalifragilisticexpialidocious!
Supercalifragilisticexpialidocious!
Supercalifragilisticexpialidocious!

A Pirate's Life

from PETER PAN

Words by Ed Penner
Music by Oliver Wallace

Verse
Moderately, with a bounce

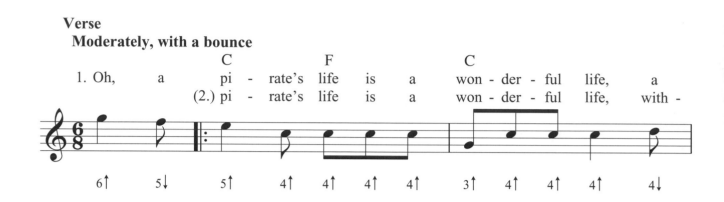

1. Oh, a pi - rate's life is a won - der - ful life, a
(2.) pi - rate's life is a won - der - ful life, with -

rov - ing o - ver the sea. Give me a ca - reer as
out a care to be - hold. You car - ry a gun and a

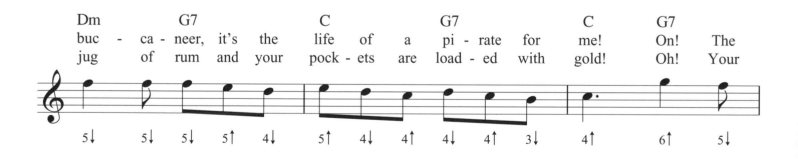

buc - ca - neer, it's the life of a pi - rate for me! On! The
jug of rum and your pock - ets are load - ed with gold! Oh! Your

life of a pi - rate for me!
pock - ets are load - ed with
2. Oh, a
gold!

Interlude

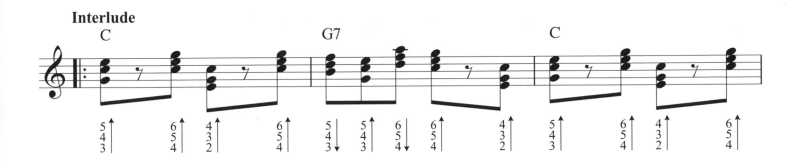

Verse

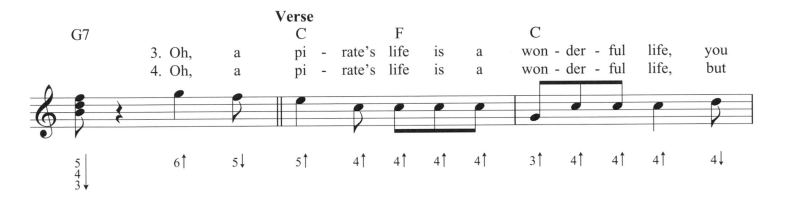

3. Oh, a pi - rate's life is a won - der - ful life, you
4. Oh, a pi - rate's life is a won - der - ful life, but

find ad - ven - ture and sport. But live ev - 'ry min - ute for
not for - ev - er they say When your neck's in a noose and you

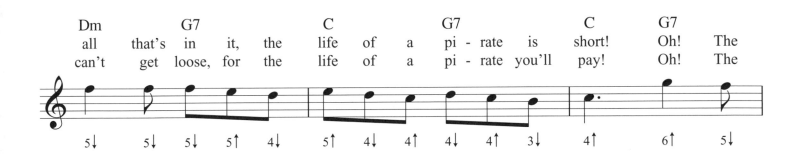

all that's in it, the life of a pi - rate is short! Oh! The
can't get loose, for the life of a pi - rate you'll pay! Oh! The

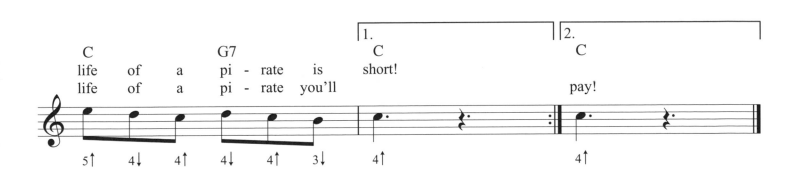

life of a pi - rate is short!
life of a pi - rate you'll pay!

Scales and Arpeggios

from THE ARISTOCATS

Words and Music by Richard M. Sherman and Robert B. Sherman

Intro
Moderately

Verse

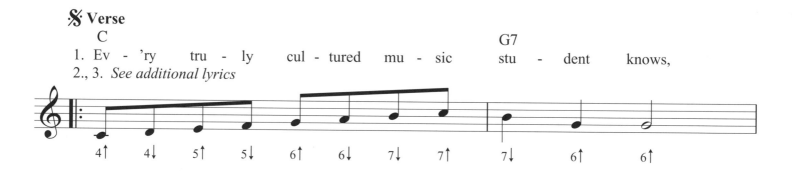

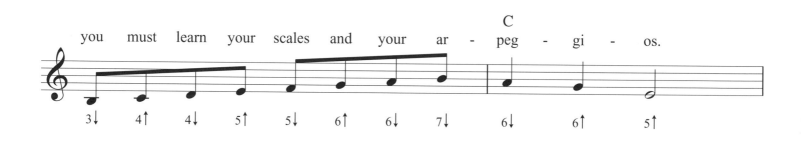

To Coda

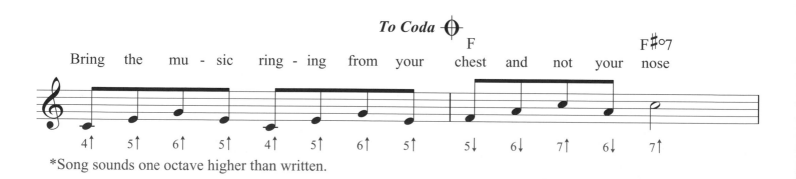

*Song sounds one octave higher than written.

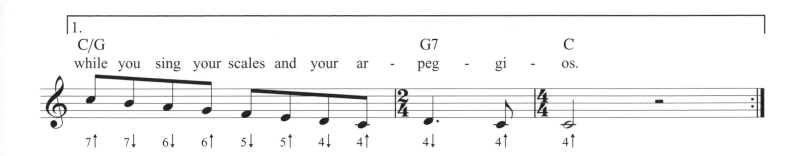

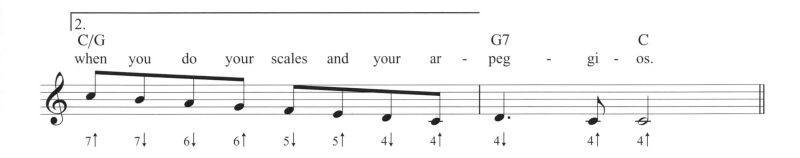

D.S. al Coda

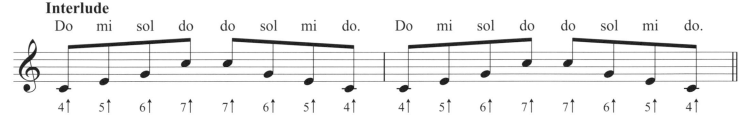

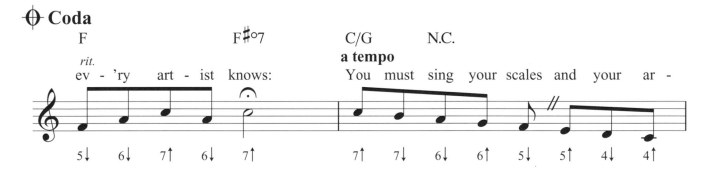

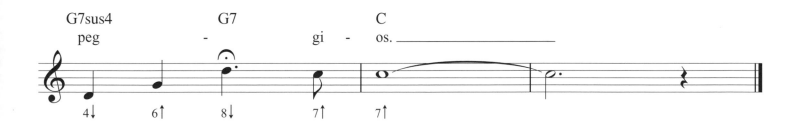

Additional Lyrics

2. If you're faithful to your daily practicing,
   You will find your progress is encouraging.
   Do mi sol mi, do mi sol mi, fa la so it goes,
   When you do your scales and your arpeggios.

3. Though at first it seems as though it doesn't show,
   Like a tree, ability will bloom and grow.
   If you're smart, you'll learn by heart what ev'ry artist knows:
   You must sing your scales and your arpeggios.

The Siamese Cat Song

from LADY AND THE TRAMP

Words and Music by Peggy Lee and Sonny Burke

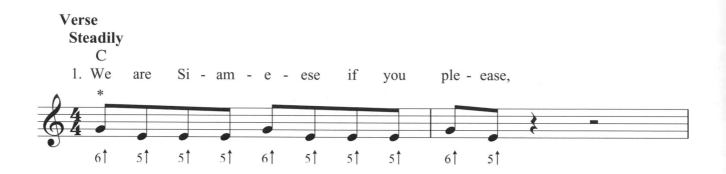

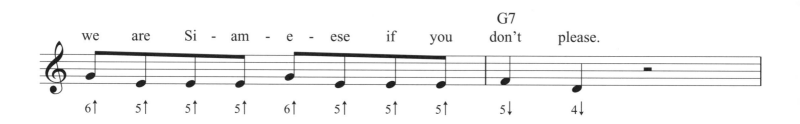

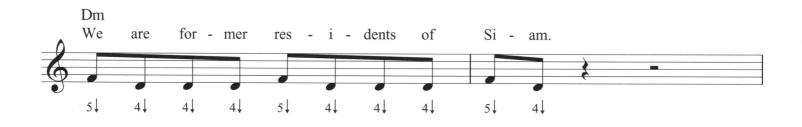

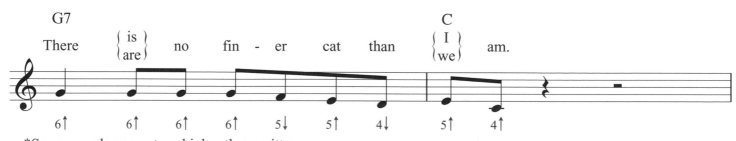

*Song sounds one octave higher than written.

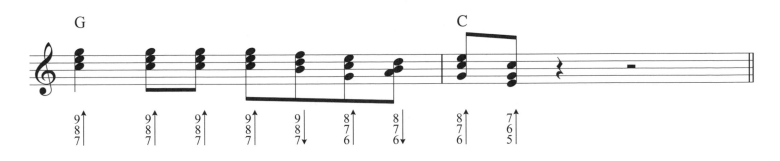

Verse

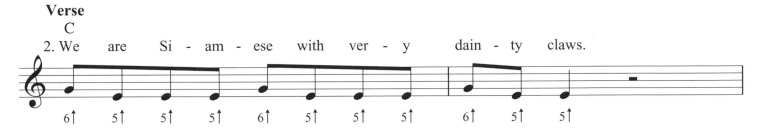

2. We are Si - am - ese with ver - y dain - ty claws.

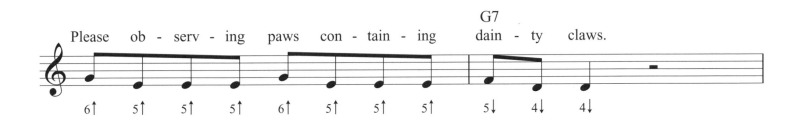

Please ob - serv - ing paws con - tain - ing dain - ty claws.

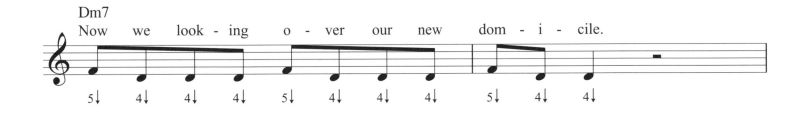

Now we look - ing o - ver our new dom - i - cile.

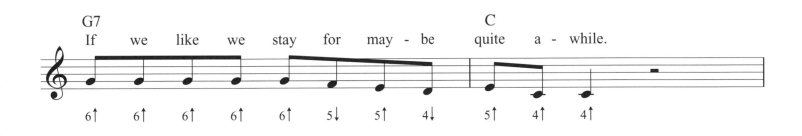

If we like we stay for may - be quite a - while.

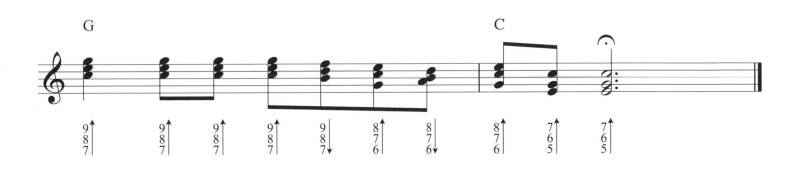

True Love's Kiss

from ENCHANTED

Music by Alan Menken
Lyrics by Stephen Schwartz

Verse
Flowing, freely

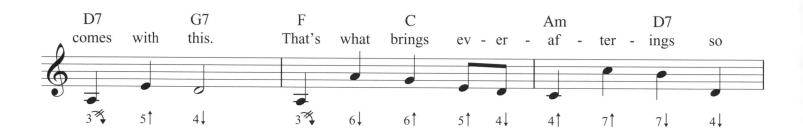

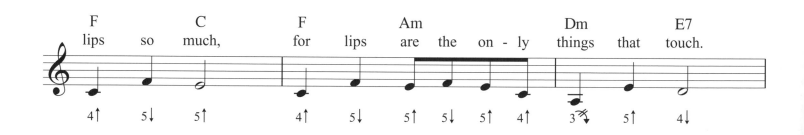

*Song sounds one octave higher than written.

just find who you love through true love's

Interlude

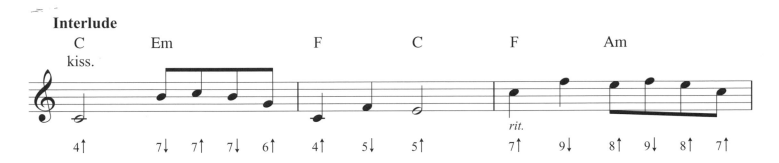

kiss.

Bridge
Light Waltz, in one

Ah, _____ ah, _____

Verse

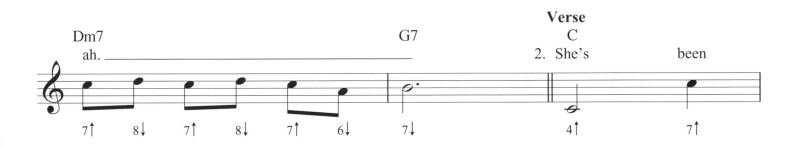

ah. _____ 2. She's been

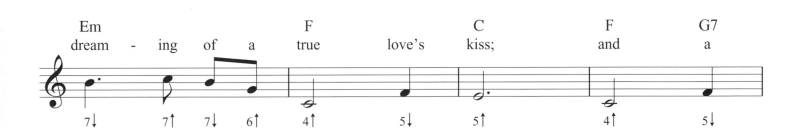

dream - ing of a true love's kiss; and a

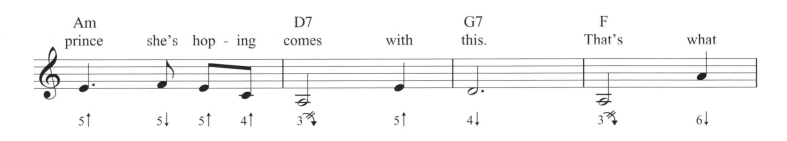

prince she's hop - ing comes with this. That's what

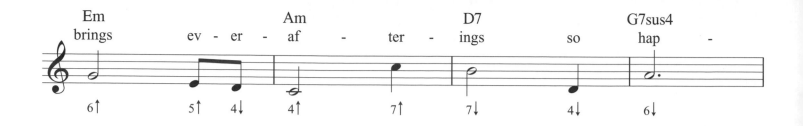

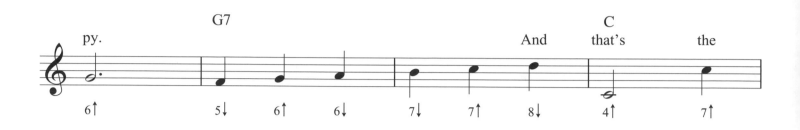

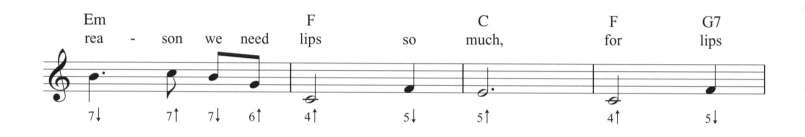

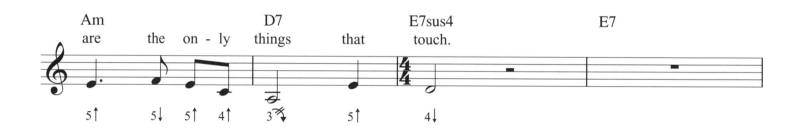

Flowing

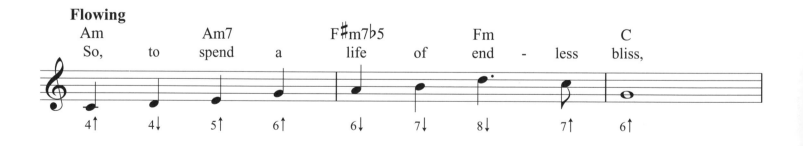

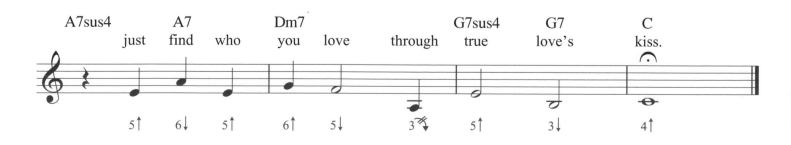

Who's Afraid of the Big Bad Wolf?

from THREE LITTLE PIGS

Words and Music by Frank Churchill
Additional Lyric by Ann Ronell

*Song sounds one octave higher than written.

had no chance to sing and _____ dance 'cause _____
slid down the chimney and, oh, by _____ jim - 'ney, in the

7↑ 7↑ 7↑ 6↑ 6↓ 7↑ 6↓ 6↑ 5↑ 5↓

Chorus

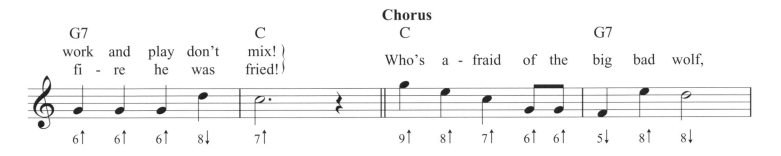

work and play don't mix! }
fi - re he was fried! }

Who's a - fraid of the big bad wolf,

6↑ 6↑ 6↑ 8↓ 7↑ 9↑ 8↑ 7↑ 6↑ 6↑ 5↓ 8↑ 8↓

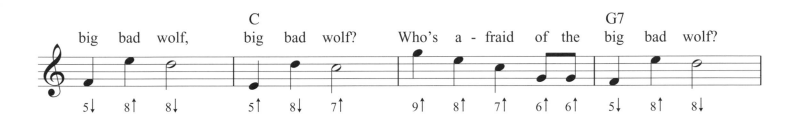

big bad wolf, big bad wolf? Who's a - fraid of the big bad wolf?

5↓ 8↑ 8↓ 5↑ 8↓ 7↑ 9↑ 8↑ 7↑ 6↑ 6↑ 5↓ 8↑ 8↓

Tra la la la la. Who's a - fraid of the big bad wolf,

6↑ 8↑ 8↓ 6↑ 7↑ 9↑ 8↑ 7↑ 6↑ 6↑ 5↓ 8↑ 8↓

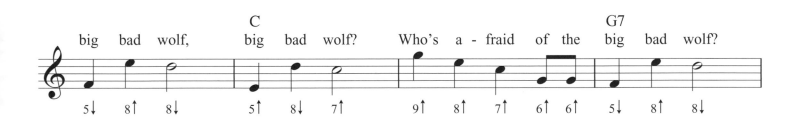

big bad wolf, big bad wolf? Who's a - fraid of the big bad wolf?

5↓ 8↑ 8↓ 5↑ 8↓ 7↑ 9↑ 8↑ 7↑ 6↑ 6↑ 5↓ 8↑ 8↓

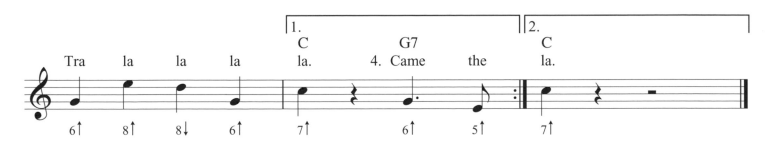

1.
Tra la la la la. 4. Came the
2.
la.

6↑ 8↑ 8↓ 6↑ 7↑ 6↑ 5↑ 7↑

A Whale of a Tale

from 20,000 LEAGUES UNDER THE SEA

Words and Music by Norman Gimbel and Al Hoffman

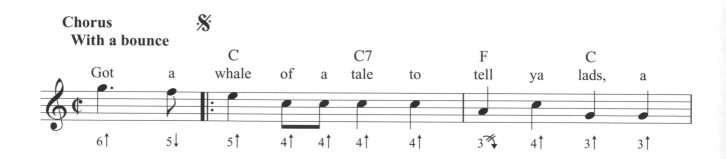

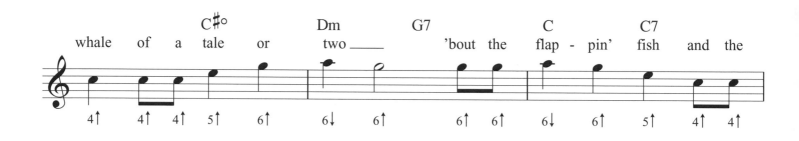

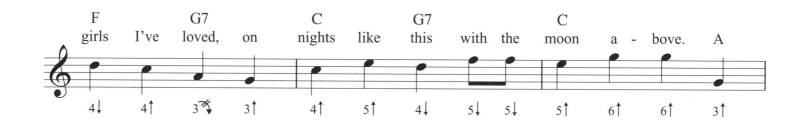

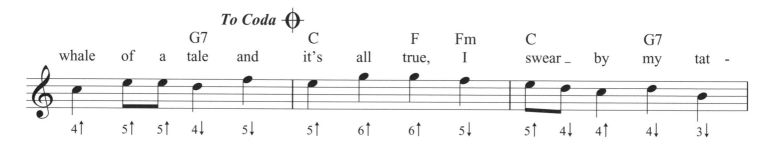

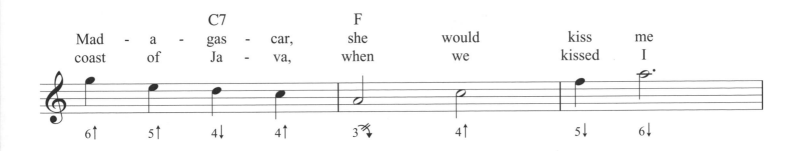

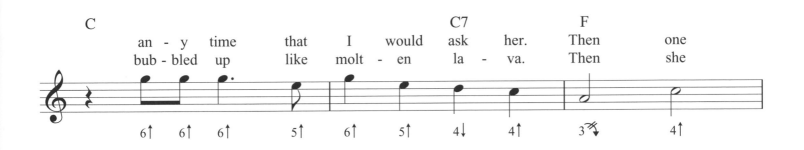

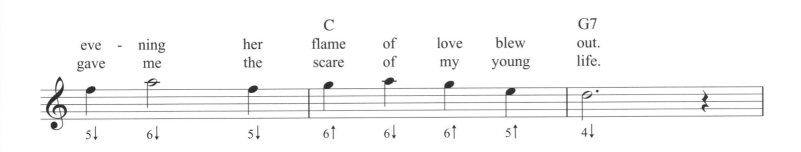

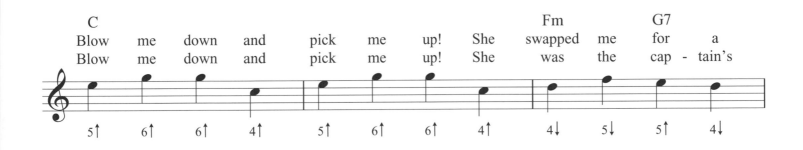

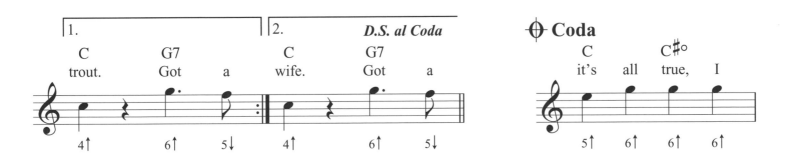

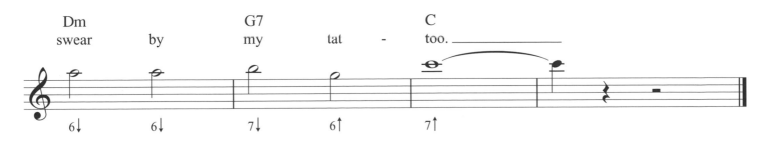

With a Smile and a Song

from SNOW WHITE AND THE SEVEN DWARFS

Words by Larry Morey
Music by Frank Churchill

Chorus
Moderately slow

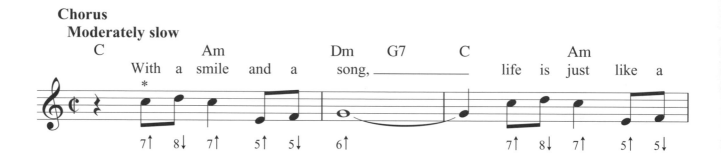

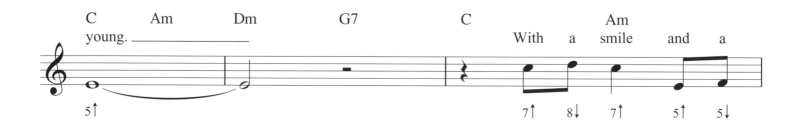

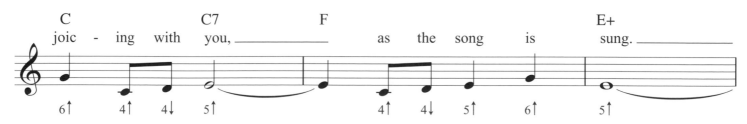

*Song sounds one octave higher than written.

Bridge

F   Fm6   C6

There's no use in grum - bling, when

4↓ 4↘ 4↓ 5↑ 4↑ 6↓ 6↓

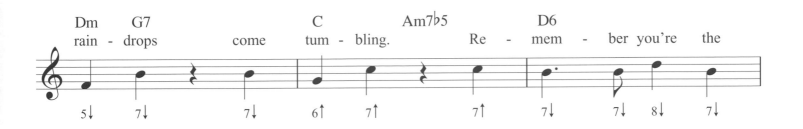

Dm   G7   C   Am7♭5   D6

rain - drops come tum - bling. Re - mem - ber you're the

5↓ 7↓ 7↓ 6↑ 7↑ 7↑ 7↓ 7↓ 8↓ 7↓

D7   Dm7   G7

one, who can fill the world with sun - shine.

6↓ 4↓ 5↑ 5↓ 5↓ 6↓ 5↓ 4↓ 6↑

Chorus

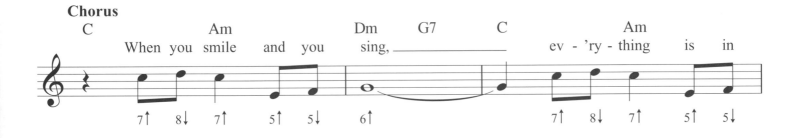

C   Am   Dm   G7   C   Am

When you smile and you sing, _____ ev - 'ry - thing is in

7↑ 8↓ 7↑ 5↑ 5↓ 6↑ 7↑ 8↓ 7↑ 5↑ 5↓

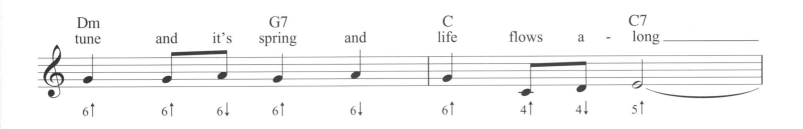

Dm   G7   C   C7

tune and it's spring and life flows a - long _____

6↑ 6↑ 6↓ 6↑ 6↓ 6↑ 4↑ 4↓ 5↑

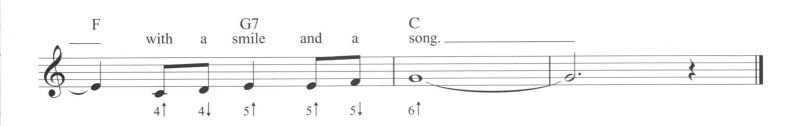

F   G7   C

with a smile and a song. _____

4↑ 4↓ 5↑ 5↑ 5↓ 6↑

Yo Ho
(A Pirate's Life for Me)

from PIRATES OF THE CARIBBEAN at Disneyland Resort® and Magic Kingdom® Park

Words by Xavier Atencio
Music by George Bruns

Chorus
In a robust manner

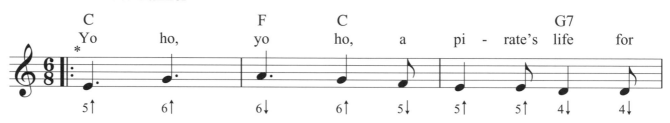

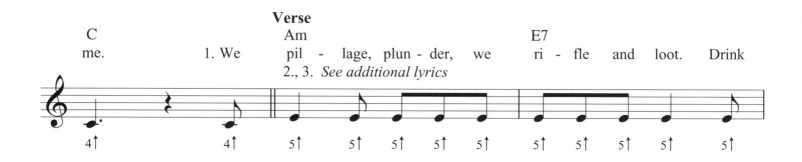

*Song sounds one octave higher than written.

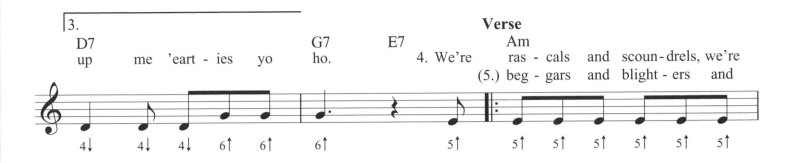

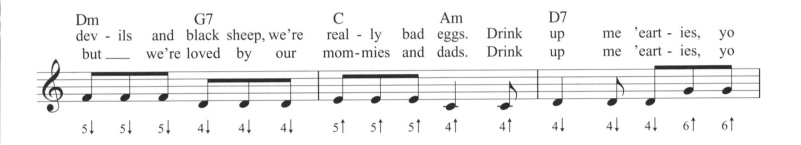

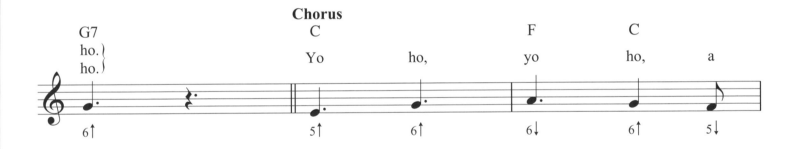

Chorus

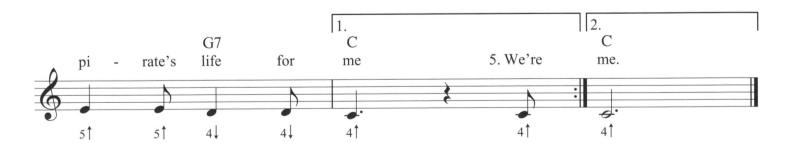

Additional Lyrics

2. We extort and pilfer, we filch and sack.
   Drink up me 'earties, yo ho.
   Maraud and embezzle and even highjack.
   Drink up me 'earties, yo ho.

3. We kindle and char and inflame and ignite.
   Drink up me 'earties, yo ho.
   We burn up the city, we're really a fright.
   Drink up me 'earties, yo ho.

Zip-A-Dee-Doo-Dah

from SONG OF THE SOUTH
Words by Ray Gilbert
Music by Allie Wrubel

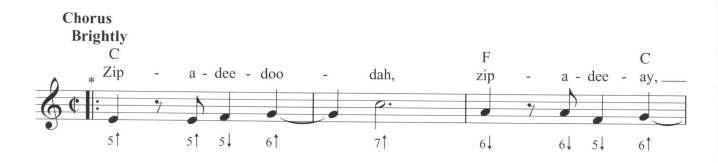

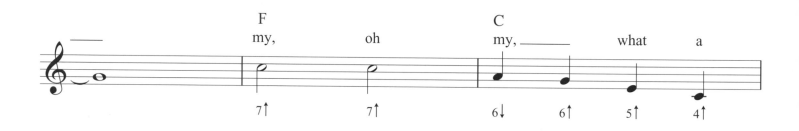

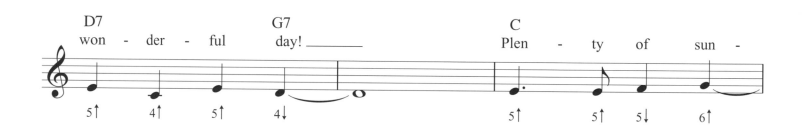

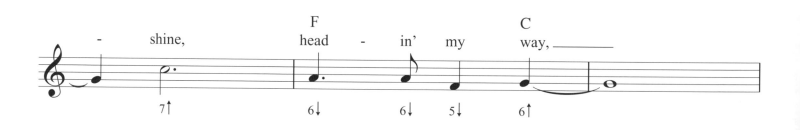

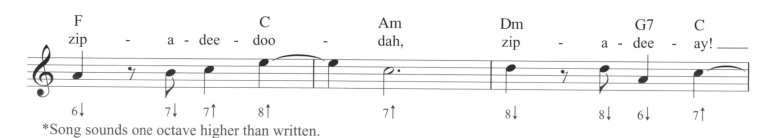

*Song sounds one octave higher than written.

Bridge

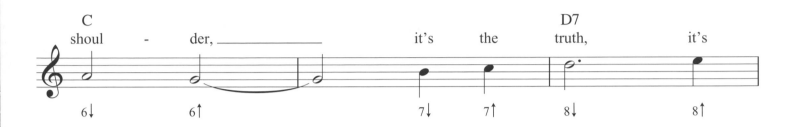

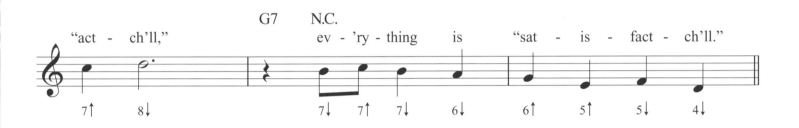

Chorus

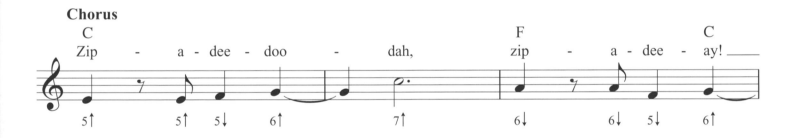

Learn To Play Today
with folk music instruction from

Hal Leonard Banjo Method – Second Edition

Authored by Mac Robertson, Robbie Clement & Will Schmid. This innovative method teaches 5-string, bluegrass style. The method consists of two instruction books and two cross-referenced supplement books that offer the beginner a carefully-paced and interest-keeping approach to the bluegrass style.

Method Book 1
00699500 Book $7.99
00695101 Book/Online Audio $16.99

Method Book 2
00699502...$7.99

Supplementary Songbooks
00699515 Easy Banjo Solos.....................................$9.99
00699516 More Easy Banjo Solos $9.99

Hal Leonard Dulcimer Method – Second Edition

by Neal Hellman

A beginning method for the Appalachian dulcimer with a unique new approach to solo melody and chord playing. Includes tuning, modes and many beautiful folk songs all demonstrated on the audio accompaniment. Music and tablature.

00699289 Book $9.99
00697230 Book/Online Audio $16.99

The Hal Leonard Complete Harmonica Method – Chromatic Harmonica

by Bobby Joe Holman

The only harmonica method to present the chromatic harmonica in 14 scales and modes in all 12 keys!

00841286 Book/Online Audio $12.99

The Hal Leonard Complete Harmonica Method – The Diatonic Harmonica

by Bobby Joe Holman

This terrific method book/CD pack specific to the diatonic harmonica covers all six positions! It contains more than 20 songs and musical examples.

00841285 Book/CD Pack.......................................$12.95

Hal Leonard Fiddle Method

by Chris Wagoner

The Hal Leonard Fiddle Method is the perfect introduction to playing folk, bluegrass and country styles on the violin. Many traditional tunes are included to illustrate a variety of techniques. The accompanying audio includes many tracks for demonstration and play-along. Covers: instrument selection and care; playing positions; theory; slides & slurs; shuffle feel; bowing; drones; playing "backup"; cross-tuning; and much more!

00311415 Book $5.99
00311416 Book/Online Audio $9.99

The Hal Leonard Mandolin Method – Second Edition

Noted mandolinist and teacher Rich Del Grosso has authored this excellent mandolin method that features great playable tunes in several styles (bluegrass, country, folk, blues) in standard music notation and tablature. The audio features play-along duets.

00699296 Book $7.99
00695102 Book/Online Audio $15.99

Hal Leonard Oud Method

by John Bilezikjian

This book teaches the fundamentals of standard Western music notation in the context of oud playing. It also covers: types of ouds, tuning the oud, playing position, how to string the oud, scales, chords, arpeggios, tremolo technique, studies and exercises, songs and rhythms from Armenia and the Middle East, and 25 audio tracks for demonstration and play along.

00695836 Book/Online Audio $12.99

Hal Leonard Ukulele Method Book 1

by Lil' Rev

This comprehensive and easy-to-use beginner's guide by acclaimed performer and uke master Lil' Rev includes many fun songs of different styles to learn and play. Includes: types of ukuleles, tuning, music reading, melody playing, chords, strumming, scales, tremolo, music notation and tablature, a variety of music styles, ukulele history and much more.

00695847 Book $6.99
00695832 Book/Online Audio $10.99

Visit Hal Leonard Online at
www.halleonard.com

Prices and availability subject to change without notice.